How to Get Along with Everyone

by Blending Personalities

Ruth McRoberts Ward

© 2019
Published in the United States by Nurturing Faith Inc., Macon GA,
www.nurturingfaith.net.

Library of Congress Cataloging-in-Publication Data is available.

ISBN: 978-1-63528-083-8

Dedication

To Jim, my dear husband/partner of 64 years,
who understands when I'm in the Intuitive world
—and lends his steady, dependable, and loving support

contents

Foreword

Ruth Ward knows what she is writing about. I know from personal observation and experience. She and her husband, Jim, have a remarkable marriage. I haven't seen their Myers-Briggs Temperament Indicator profiles, but I assure you, they are not two peas in a pod. They have learned to love each other more deeply because they accept each other as a person of great value whom God has entrusted with a special outlook and temperament. And, they have learned to see others as special people— at least some of whom have different outlooks and temperaments.

Ruth Ward has established meaningful friendships and deep relationships with people of multitudinous backgrounds, ethnicities, social and financial strata, and ages. She is almost a magician when it comes to helping people, married and not, learn how to communicate with others with great understanding and appreciation. She doesn't just tell people to get along; she tells them how to get along.

When I was a student in seminary and Ruth was the administrative assistant to the dean of students, she helped bridge a great gap between the dean and me. She helped me come to appreciate the dean, and the dean to realize I might not be quite as bad as some of my actions would otherwise appear. The dean and I became good friends after Ruth interceded.

Helping folks know how to get along is one of God's gifts to Ruth. She has worked diligently to gain further knowledge and skill to help hundreds of people understand how to relate with others unlike themselves. Now she uses that gift to help others benefit from her abilities and labor.

Anyone who reads—no, not just reads but devours—this book will be a far better, understanding, accepting person, even folks who may be difficult in just about any manner. Read it, study it, and implement its truths and you will be a better person with better relationships.

Lynn Clayton
Former editor, Louisiana Baptist Message

Preface

Most people, regardless of their age, want to be respected for who they are and appreciated for what they do. However, when how we act or speak does not match others' expectations, we may experience feelings of inadequacy, anger, and guilt, which spawn resentments.

In counseling sessions, I hear comments such as "I just can't live up to his expectations" or "I've done everything I can think of and she still doesn't approve of me." Another common theme is "I would like to tell people how I feel, but I can't stand conflict." Or, "Yes, they're my children but I don't understand where they're coming from." Similarly, "Why is it that I say 'yes' when I mean 'no'? I resent the person who asked me, yet I feel guilty if I don't comply." Then there's the husband who declares "If she would just follow my schedule, we'd have no problems."

Unresolved anger and stored resentment often seed depression and other illnesses. These emotional upheavals block good communication and destroy creativity.

Ironically, most guilt-producing expectations are either unfair, unspoken, unrealistic, childish, or selfish. Ideally, healthy anger assists in identifying the sources of our guilt feelings. When understood, appreciated, and rightly used, anger becomes a friend rather than a foe.

Understanding differing patterns of temperament is the key to blending personalities, ultimately producing and/or improving communication, easing tensions and paving the way to get along with everyone, even the people we barely like.

How to Get Along with Everyone by Blending Personalities intends to meet your personal and communication needs. The Myers-Briggs Temperament Indicator (MBTI) provides such a catapult.

Maybe you've heard about or actually taken the MBTI without an in-depth interpretation, and therefore have no idea how to get the good out of the questionnaire you took. This book simplifies the concept, making it easy to include the skill in your stash of communication tips. Testimonials in chapter 2 from friends, clients, and family members attest to sweetening their relationships by applying principles from the MBTI.

My extended family—numbering more than 80—has used MBTI communication insight for 30-plus years. Several of us are involved in counseling of one kind or another, so MBTI is a household term. For those of you who know lots about the MBTI, I use temperament, type, and personality interchangeably to keep it simple.

Blending Personalities pinpoints analogies between differing temperament types. Many of these suggestions parallel the ways we would cultivate flower species in a garden with careful, skillful, daily attention. Even though each variety of flower possesses unique qualities, all plants have similar needs and face common problems as they grow together to achieve a healthy, clean, and beautiful garden. They struggle against pesky insects, compete with greedy weeds, deal with a lack of water, resist destructive winds and foul weather, and submit to necessary pruning.

The same applies as we embrace our unique design and appreciate others' designs. This inclusive attitude marks the path to unity and harmony by merely honing the skills of communication. The 16 unique personal profiles guarantee the journey will be simple and fun as you claim your true identity.

This book offers guidelines for nurturing relationships with your children, partners, co-workers, extended family, and neighbors. The ideas presented stem from my *Blending Temperaments* book that focuses on marriage counseling and enrichment conferences that my husband, Jim, and I conducted.

(Since confidentiality is essential, names and situations have been altered to preserve the anonymity of clients, family, and friends.)

Acknowledgments

To my brother, Chaplain Marvin (Mac) McRoberts,
who introduced the MBTI to me some 30 years ago:
he projected it "would change my life"—and he was right

To my son, Roger, for guidelines and excellent advice

To family members, especially my granddaughter Laura, her husband
Kurt Gordon and my granddauther Kathryn DiVirgilins,
who were constant technical advisors

To clients, extended family. and friends who submitted testimonials

To Jackie Riley, my editor-friend, for her generous
encouragement and direction

CHAPTER 1

Self-Esteem: Recognizing Our Differences

Let us therefore make every effort to do what leads to
peace and to mutual edification.
Romans 14:19

Does anyone think you're strange? Do you? Few of us have little idea who we really are down deep. I didn't know until I was 40 why I behaved and thought so differently from my mate, siblings, good friends, co-workers, and young children. I soon became amazingly aware that a few of us were on the same page. Although that observation was mind-boggling, I discovered quickly that being different was not strange at all.

My goal is to put a feather in everyone's cap. When you discover who you really are, you'll never want to trade places with anyone else. I'm confident you won't regret the time invested in reading this book and enhancing your communication skills. Healthy self-image is the ticket to open, honest communication and harmony for which people really thirst. Lack of skill in self-expression on the part of ourselves and others limits our ability for that clear communication and harmony. With improved self-esteem we gain confidence in positive interactions and relationships with others. We're going to have a great time unraveling all this marvelous information.

Most of us have known for years that low self-esteem can be a serious burden. Long ago a Gallup poll declared that it is the number-one problem in America. Help is needed in understanding ourselves and others in order to improve our quality of life by getting along with everyone. Healthy self-esteem exudes from a reservoir within that generates a sense of comfortable confidence as we converse. Even though we each have an inborn personality and character traits, our moods are affected by the people around us.

Before moving on to the interpretation, I want readers to know that one of the strongest inspirations for presenting this study is to bring understanding, relief, and respect to Head-Logic females and Heart-Logic males—the minorities in decision making—and specifically to correct a major part of society's insistence that men are strong, stoic, practical, decision makers whereas females are weak, weepy, indecisive, and wrong. Throughout this study my goal is to assist readers to understand, accept, respect, and encourage Heart-Logic males and Head-Logic females to celebrate their unique design.

As stated in my book, *Self-Esteem: Gift from God,* "For a man to discover that he is tenderhearted or a woman that she is coldhearted can be a disturbing, yet helpful, revelation toward self-acceptance. Understanding that these traits are actually innate allows individuals to identify their true preference and to strengthen the weaker side of their nature."

The following study will not only nurture your self-esteem but also will considerably improve your communication skills. As a bonus, it will provide a candid, fresh, and flattering portrait of yourself and your partner, co-workers, children, and acquaintances—anyone who crosses your path. You not only will find personal relief but also will be able to encourage others. As you consider the testimonials from clients, friends, and family who have become aware of their personality type and successfully applied the insight at home and work and socially, I trust you'll do yourself a favor and keep going. Treat yourself with this life-changing information. I promise: you'll never be the same.

Boy, Are We Ever Different!

- Men, do you ever wonder why some guys have little interest in simple maintenance on their automobiles and procrastinate making small repairs around the house?
- Ladies, is it puzzling that your sister enjoys doing handicrafts and your friend delights in house cleaning, while neither activity interests you much?
- Whatever your gender, do you ever wonder why some people rarely speak up and others never keep quiet?
- Those of you who say yes when you mean no and tear up at any sad account, would you like help in understanding your emotions that ebb and flow constantly?
- Parents, do you ever wonder why your teenage daughter keeps a messy room, though you've trained her to do better? Why is it that the same offspring or her brother, sometimes stubborn as a mule, ignores your lists and helpful reminders?
- Teachers, do you ever wonder why some students are assertive and self-confident while others—even siblings from the same home—resist leadership and dialogue or why some students possess self-discipline in turning in assignments while others struggle with meeting deadlines?
- Do you ever wonder why your partner bends over backwards to aid others yet resists your simple requests for help or why he withholds details of his work day or "people news" unless the subject comes up?

The majority of strange actions and responses can be understood by reviewing the four preferences:

1. Social
2. Information Gathering
3. Decision Making
4. Lifestyle

Each preference offers two options. Since all our basic traits are unique gifts, knowing one's personality preferences in each area removes the need to apologize for how one prefers to think and act and also produces patience toward others who prefer to function in opposite ways.

For some odd reason, we often find ourselves surrounded by people—even our biological children or natural parents—who think and behave differently from us. The normal reaction is to label another's unusual ideas and behaviors as insecurities, immaturities, inferiorities, arrogance, weakness, laziness, snobbishness, or selfishness. All are negative terms resulting in upsetting our silent expectations. Complete opposites to us exist, and they're normal too.

We are made for human relationships, and relationships depend on healthy communication. Being content with ourselves should relieve the pressure on others to love and value us. It behooves us, therefore, to acquaint ourselves with the personality preferences of those with whom we rub shoulders at home, work, school, etc. not only to help us cope with others but, more importantly, to avoid resentments and neutralize expectations.

Following is a shortened explanation of the Myers-Briggs Type Indicator that I have used successfully in counseling and seminars for more than 38 years. My book *Self-Esteem: Gift from God* describes each area in more detail.

Interpretation of MBTI

Social Preference: Inner and Outer Worlds
I vs. E. (Introversion vs. Extroversion)

Privacy-prone introverts. About 25 percent of the population is decidedly turned inward, having a high preference for privacy rather than people, and peace and quiet rather than noise and confusion. The remainder of the population is extroverted to some degree, possessing a greater capacity for crowds, noise, and confusion and a lower need for privacy. The world in general seems more receptive to extroverts, which often puts their opposites at a distinct disadvantage.

"When my wife's feet hit the floor in the morning," an introvert shared, "her tongue is activated—or is it tongues?" Some introverts cleverly stay in bed until their extroverted mate and children have cleared out, so they can dress and eat breakfast in silence.

Introverts avoid crowded gatherings, preferring one-on-one relationships. They usually do not choose to converse unless they are comfortable and the group is small, while most extroverts have little problem engaging strangers in conversation or speaking up in public.

Introverts generally weigh words and ponder before they speak—"mind editing," I call it—which reduces verbal blunders but produces slower responses. "By the time I sift and decide what I want to say," an introverted businessman complained, "someone else has either verbalized what I intended to say or has moved on to another subject. Frustrating."

"Not having the opportunity to put our two cents in," a quality control employee defended, "we introverts are thought to be dull, bored, mad, or sad—or worse yet, stuck up. We're usually none of those. We have plenty to say if people would just give us an opening."

Many introverts agree that people often ask them if everything is okay. Without realizing it, an introvert's silence and sobriety—often misinterpreted as confidence and knowledge—can be intimidating to extroverts. A familiar proverb says, "Even a fool is thought wise if he keeps silent" (Prov. 17:28).

Introverts are astonished to learn that others are frightened of them. "People have no idea how I shudder inside," a successful businessperson shared. "I'm never completely comfortable giving reports to large groups."

"We fear someone is going to ask a question we can't or don't want to answer," a small group of introverts wrote on their report. "We prefer to have plenty of time to think about our answer because we want our information to be not only pertinent but also accurate."

Because introverts have a tendency to bottle up their anger and other emotions, they suffer more often with depression. Their careful calculations can result in pessimism. Although introverts seem to be stoic, they are usually quite sensitive, feel hurts and slights, and care deeply for others. Introverts are actually two people—one at home and a different one away from home.

People-prone extroverts. About 75 percent of the general population is decidedly extroverted and need people, noise, and conversation. Extroverts generally speak first, then think, and often attempt to erase some of what they just said. They rely on what I call "ear editing," and have to intentionally learn to think first.

"I really don't know what I'm thinking until I hear myself talk," many extroverts confess. "I talk until I think of something to say," Garrison Keillor, a popular monologist, quipped. Extroverts acknowledge uncomfortably that many times they "open mouth and insert foot."

Extroverts, for the most part, test their statements by ear as well as the looks on listeners' faces. They readily voice their opinions, volunteering how they feel, how much weight they've lost, if they got a speeding ticket, or what's happened so far today. They openly discuss projects they are working on without being prompted. Many extroverts admit that they are amazed at what and how much they say. In fact, extroverts are attracted to introverts just because they are good listeners.

Since introverts test statements before they ever leave their brains, their misstatements remain unspoken. "It seems like you extroverts are afraid of no one and never at a loss for words," a workshop group of introverts concluded. "We really envy those abilities."

"Even though we may exude a fearless, self-confident impression," an extrovert replied, "we do get nervous and bandy-legged at times. We just don't let on." However, extroverts' optimism, self-confidence, and ability not to take themselves or setbacks too seriously greatly redeem their wordiness.

"Extroverts keep us introverts from being so boring," a small group of the latter observed. "They also are good at easing awkward situations with their humorous banter."

Some strong extroverts feel obligated to fill the airwaves because they assume that lulls in conversation are just as annoying to others as to them. Not so.

An extrovert's tendency to finish a slow speaker's sentences (because the extrovert prefers immediate responses and also has something more to say) irritates both introverts and other less confident or stammering extroverts. "Extroverts almost choke on what they know," a workshop member shared.

Because extroverts require exposure to many people and little privacy, being alone is as distasteful to some of them as being with too many people is to introverts. Some simply must have conversation and/or people around them most of the day or they become restless or suffer from boredom and loneliness. Usually these feelings last only until they get around people again. Extroverts can and must learn to edit their voluminous verbiage, if not for the benefit of others, then, for their own protection to trim away the need for "I spoke out of turn" statements. I often suggest as a practical goal that they cut in half what they want to say.

Learning to listen is a skill worth cultivating. On the other hand, if introverts would smile a bit more and risk jumping into conversations by announcing that "I have something to say," they would destroy some of extroverts' wrong assumptions about them and would bless their communities with their unique humor, opinions, and profound ideas.

In my opinion, gathered from years of counseling, the most distinguishing contrast between Introversion and Extroversion is the effect people have on them. Being with people drains introverts but charges up extroverts.

The biggest favor that extroverts can bestow on introverts is to request their opinions and grant them privacy and recouping time. Introverts should learn to inform extroverts when their ears are weary. Neither way of reacting to the outer world is superior. Most normal people are a blend of both Introversion and Extroversion. To be totally extroverted or introverted might indicate serious emotional or social problems.

Information Gathering: Facts vs. Ideas
S vs. N (Sensing vs. Intuitive)

Since the letter "I" has already been used to refer to Introversion, "N" will be used to designate Intuition. Going forward, I'll adjust the spelling to iNtuition to facilitate your use of the letter "N" for Intuition.

Two preferences used simultaneously influence life's direction: information gathering and decision making. (The latter will be covered in the next section.)

The two main sources for information gathering are Sensing and iNtuition. Our sensory systems—what we see, hear, taste, touch, and feel—collect and catalog black-and-white facts and figures that aid survival in the conscious world.

iNtuition supplies abstract ideas and possibilities that are especially helpful in problem solving and design. For good balance, we need to embrace both Sensing and iNtuition and learn to blend the information gathered from each. We accomplish that automatically, but on an individual basis one source is easier and more appealing to use while the other requires a disciplined effort

Feet on the ground. Those who strongly prefer sensory information gathering—75 percent of the population—discover that their "observers" are always on. They automatically pick up physical data with their eyes, ears, nose, touch, and tongue. Cataloguing physical facts, figures, dates, and details comes naturally. Sensing types pride themselves on being accurate and exact and are perplexed when others forget the things they can remember so easily. In arguments, Sensing people can destroy iNtuitives with facts and are sometimes characterized as having a feet-on-the-ground approach to life. They give stability to our world.

Those who prefer the Sensing preference are generally attracted to hands-on careers and involvements. Once they master a product, service, or technique, they enjoy repeating and polishing the process, which results in perfection, high production, and growth. Their tolerance for repetition keeps them from being bored and gives them a healthy capacity for routine.

"Routine is necessary to make the world go 'round," a Sensing seminar group agreed.

"We earn tenure awards because we stick with what we like," one member added.

"I like to know what is expected of me and appreciate having all the supplies I need on hand before I begin a project," another shared.

"For people like us, what we are working on is what we are thinking about. That's why we make fewer mistakes. We are proud of what we accomplish."

"We like our ability to use common sense and to follow directions. Why have directions if you're not going to follow them?"

"We dislike radical change, preferring the simplicity of gradual adjustments. Please give us plenty of time to digest facts before pressing for decisions. We aren't slow or dull, just more accurate."

The rest of the world sometimes takes for granted Sensing people's contributions toward keeping things comfortable, solvent, beautiful, and moving smoothly. This group is conscious of today, yet fervently aware of yesterday. They instinctively check with past experience before making decisions—which explains some of their reluctance to try something again

"We like to keep life simple," the Sensing group explained. "One thing at a time," "Don't fix it if it isn't broken," and "We've always done it this way" are statements that could describe their general approach. The Sensing segment faces problems when encountered.

The world is greatly indebted to the many Sensing people who faithfully serve as bankers, doctors, nurses, mechanics, bookkeepers, administrators, secretaries, teachers, factory workers, salespersons, and in dozens of other product-related service careers. However, many of these people have also found their way into iNtuitive careers and responsibilities where they have contributed significantly. The iNtuitive world benefits from their repetitive, steady hands.

Head in the clouds. People who prefer the iNtuitive way of gathering information number 25 percent of the general population. They are the dreamers and are more alive to the unknown world of possibility thinking, design, hunches, and "what might be." Their constant jumble of ideas seems to leave little room or time for facts, figures, and practical concerns.

Perhaps the stereotypical absent-minded professors best typify this head-in-the-clouds approach. "We remember the facts that we think are important or will support our case," they reason, "but we prefer to find solutions through our possibility thinking. We love solving problems, and we like to solve our own before they arrive."

Because iNtuitives prefer using mental processes, they are often impatient with performing repetitious physical activities. For example, they may find the routine of cutting grass, auto and home maintenance, housework, bookkeeping, and the like not only boring but also unfulfilling.

iNtuitives are usually surprised to learn that their incessant questions may intimidate a Sensor, especially one who assumes that interrogators are smart. "Maybe he's after my job," a Sensing person worries, not realizing that curiosity and an insatiable hunger to learn new things prompts an iNtuitive to probe for subtle information.

Whereas Sensing people like to produce a useful product, system, or service, iNtuitives prefer to improve the same. However, once they learn the ropes, unless there's lots of variety and change, they often lose interest and crave new goals and challenges.

The goal of iNtuitives is to have a goal—or four. They want to be involved in projects that are bigger than themselves. If nothing is left to master, their interest wanes. This explains why some people have had many unrelated jobs or earned several degrees by the time they reach retirement years. "We admit that we're jacks of all trades and masters of none," an iNtuitive shared with the group. "We'd really like to display one thing that we do well. But alas, who can see inside our minds?" And it's not uncommon to hear a 40-plus-year-old iNtuitive dream, "You know what I want to do when I grow up?"

iNtuitives prefer that each day be different so as to break routine, still another reason why they find time-clock jobs distasteful. To neutralize the boredom in repetitive jobs, many create mind games. Today, thanks to Internet capabilities, working from home has become a reality for many iNtuitves who endeavor to eliminate time-consuming commutes and to lessen auto expense and the inevitability of empty gas tanks and flat tires.

Because iNtuitives have the ability to see all around and beyond an event—maybe 10 years or more down the road—they may come across as preoccupied, flaky, or distant. They are certainly known for chasing rabbit trails in meetings. "Head in the clouds" people struggle to pare down their ideas and reach decision time. "It's true that 'the lights are on but nobody's home' certainly describes us at times," an iNtuitive surmised, "but, honestly, we are busy in there. We normally have several conversations with ourselves going on in our head."

"Looking beyond the present situation of details and seeing the big picture appeal to us," an iNtuitive explained to his group. "We admit that we spend too much time in indecision or going in circles, where we miss a lot of what's going on, but what's going to happen tomorrow is much more exciting to us than what's going on right now. We prefer to prevent problems. Appreciate us for our ideas, and we'll be happy campers."

Although iNtuitives are known for stirring the pot, the world is indebted to them for systems analyses, counseling, writing, research, teaching, preaching, and other careers that involve theory, behavior, and improving mental, spiritual, and emotional heath. The Sensing world is richer for having a few dreaming iNtuitives on committees and teams who are not afraid to make radical changes for the sake of improvement.

Remember: everyone is a blend of both the Sensing and iNtuitive preferences, leaning more one way than the other. However, for balance each must consult and use both preferences as situations demand. Our goals should be not to think alike but together and to celebrate differences rather than criticize.

Decision Making:
T vs. F (Thinking / Head-Logic vs. Feeling / Heart-Logic)

Two considerations, head and heart, influence our decision making and determine the method we will use in most situations. Head-Logic practical decisions based on cold facts are Thinking-oriented. Emotional, Heart-Logic decisions involving people and emotions are Feeling-oriented.

The general population is split 50/50 on Thinking and Feeling. For overall social development and stability, a person needs occasionally to exercise and blend both methods of decision making. But again, each individual tends to trust and depend on one method more than the other and therefore finds it easier and more natural to use.

Do what's practical (T). Head-Logic Thinkers are often regarded as cold, inconsiderate, stubborn, selfish, impatient, unforgiving, or all-business. They rarely admit their decisions are wrong unless irrefutable facts prove them so.

Because they are not driven to please others and maintain harmony, they consider only what seems most practical, fair, economical, or efficient, rather than how others might feel about it. Thinkers expect approval of their decisions, and silence from another means approval. Thinkers struggle to give others approval because it's difficult to give what they don't need.

Head-Logic Thinkers base their decisions on cause-and-effect practicalities, preferring to make situation-based choices. Their first answer is no, and their second answer is no—unless they are fed feasible facts that change the issue. They trust their own decisions most and want others to respect their judgment powers and appreciate them afterwards.

Thinkers are wise to be aware that logical decisions are not always the best ones, that often harmonious relationships prevail over practicality. Conversely, Head-Logic Thinkers are capable of making impersonal, unpopular, distasteful, and disappointing decisions that actually relieve their Feeling counterparts who need support in making difficult decisions.

We accept that tough, logical decisions keep the world upright, rational, and stable. Although Feeling people are often intimidated, upset, and even frightened by Thinkers, they are indebted to Thinkers for making difficult decisions and maintaining security.

"We do not make decisions out of spite or intentionally to take advantage of others' weaknesses," a Thinking workshop group defended. "We just prefer to make reasonable decisions that conserve time, money, and energy. Sure, we respect peace and harmony, but we function very well without them."

"We do have feelings," a Thinking group countered. "We just don't allow emotions to dictate decisions. Our hurts usually don't linger, because we think through the whole situation and forget it. But we do need help in acknowledging and understanding our feelings."

The complaint often leveled at Thinkers is their reluctance to pass on news they consider irrelevant to the situation. "My mate never shares anything about work," his companion said. "I learn more from a secondhand phone conversation." When confronted with his negligence in this respect, the mate calmly replied: "When I spend 8-10 hours in the jungle of jangled nerves, do you think I want to come home and go over all of it again and load you up with all that garbage, too? I consider my family a separate priority and refuse to let my career consume my attention when I'm home."

Thinkers have a tendency to store information for later reference, drawing upon it only if the subject related to those facts surfaces. On the other hand, Feeling men and women voluntarily transfer such tidbits as "Guess what I heard today!" to anyone they feel would be interested.

Therefore, Thinkers' friends and family are often incensed and hurt to be the last to learn pertinent data. The Feeling (Heart-Logic) people tend to measure their importance by the amount of information passed on from their significant other. Thinkers can develop a sharing attitude by making notes throughout the day of events and news that can be shared with their "tenderhearted" counterparts.

Do what feels comfortable (F). Half of the general population finds Feeling, or Heart-Logic, decisions more natural than Head-Logic ones. Emotional Feeling decision makers are strongly influenced by their own and other peoples' needs and opinions. Ranking more important than saving money, time, or energy, maintaining harmony, receiving others' approval, and sidestepping arguments take precedence with Feeling deciders. They avoid confrontations because they dislike criticism of themselves—a weakness that needs to be faced.

A significant characteristic of Heart-Logic tenderhearted people is their preference for making choices that benefit others. They tend to choose careers or jobs that affect the everyday lives of others, such as sales, social work, medical, teaching, and service endeavors.

Before the softhearted make a decision, they consider how others will receive it. For example, "I know you counted on my being home this evening, but I have to work late. I'm very sorry." Silence to Feelers means disapproval—you shouldn't do it, buy it, etc.

Tenderhearted men and women are naturally apologetic and hate to hurt feelings. They are skilled at gift-wrapping or explaining their statements. They may preface their opinions with such conciliatory remarks as "You may disagree with me, but…" They generally choose the flexible word "feel" more often than the decisive word "think."

Feelers have a habit of dancing all around a subject before getting to the facts of the issue at hand. This seems to be a major irritant to Thinkers. "Just tell me what happened, what you mean, what you're afraid of," the latter urge.

Although they dislike disagreements and fights, Feelers are most often the ones involved in scraps, because their sensitive emotions easily erupt over hurt feelings, rejections, and slights. Many cry easily in response to either good or bad news.

Because Feelers do not want to disappoint anyone, they do many things they don't want to do, saying yes when they mean no. They treat others as they would like to be treated and expect others to return the favor. Many people take advantage of Feelers' generosity of time, money, and energy. Feelers get hurt first, then angry when their gifts or favors are overlooked or unappreciated.

When others do not reciprocate, softhearted men and women may experience anger, jealousy, self-pity, or resentment. Feeling deciders are likely to put high demands on others and then suffer emotional hurt when their expectations are ignored or unfulfilled.

Feelers function better with approval, affirmation, appreciation, acceptance, and affection (the "A" words)—which Thinkers are reticent in giving, since trust and respect suit them fine. "It's difficult to give what you don't need," they plead. Conversely, Feelers find it difficult to withhold from others what they like to give.

Feelers constantly battle mixed emotions since making decisions based on impersonal data is a difficult assignment. Feeling deciders want everyone to like them, even those people they dislike and have difficulty living or working with.

Just as Thinkers can benefit from understanding the Feeling deciders' perspective, so can the latter benefit from consulting with Thinkers before making final decisions. Our world is indebted to Feeling males and females for insisting on and fighting for peace and harmony. They are often the ones who give a person "one more chance," cold facts notwithstanding.

It has been reliably documented that 60 percent of men and 40 percent of women prefer Head-Logic Thinking decision making. Conversely, 60 percent of females and 40 percent of males prefer Feeling Heart-Logic decisions along with 40 percent of males. (The special problems of Head-Logic females and Heart-Logic males will be covered in a later chapter.)

Lifestyle:
J vs. P (Judging / Structure vs. Perceptive / Spontaneous)

In my experience, using the MBTI words Judging and Perceptive has been somewhat confusing and hampers clear understanding. Many clients freeze at the word judgment, assuming it means judgmental—connoting negative and critical. To utilize the excellent Myers-Briggs Type table, we must use its four-letter identification key, so, I have substituted the words Structure and Organized in place of Judging but have retained the MBTI letter "J".

Perceptive is also a good word choice for lifestyle, but clients relate more readily to Spontaneous or Unstructured when describing lifestyle. I have kept the letter "P" by using the "P" in sPontaneous. So, in this study I use "J" (Structured or Organized) and "P" (sPontaneous or Unstructured).

Differences in lifestyle preferences present a basic source of communication problems and can explain much of the friction between any two people who share a relationship, including mates, parent and child, close friends, co-workers and bosses.

When the two lifestyle preferences are understood, they not only make good sense and ease much tension, but also the differences are often a source of amusement. For example, one couple who had been trying to change each other for years now just shrug their shoulders and laugh about differences that once were a cause of discord.

Keep on schedule. People who prefer a Structured or Organized lifestyle (J) are work-oriented. They like to get necessary projects finished before they play. In fact, they cannot enjoy leisure unless work is complete. Some Structured people have to be away from home in order to play.

Structured / Organized people usually make lists and relish crossing off the items as they are completed. Some say they even put "lunch" on the list so they can cross it off.

"J" people often judge the success of their day by how much they accomplished. "Work, it must be done" is their motto. "Let's get started so we can get it over with" is a favorite directive for the Structured and Organized. Not only do they love to work, but almost everything they do is regarded as or called work—both jobs they like and those they dislike. Quite often, they tackle distasteful jobs first. Some say that they work at playing. They love the word work.

Making appointments and scheduling give Structured people the organized outline needed for their lives. Without a planned agenda, they may feel insecure. In fact, Structured people are likely to waste a day that has not been planned, though they hate themselves afterwards. What they often forget is that everyone needs a certain amount of throwaway time in order to avoid burnout.

"We don't mind Structured people doing their thing," a sPontaneous seminar participant shared, "but we dislike it when they try to organize us." The group laughed when he added, "We have a different strategy for getting things done."

Typical was a remark overheard at a family campout consisting of mostly Structured relatives: "We have a free day; let's schedule it," a Structured uncle said. "Why ruin a perfectly beautiful day like that?" a sPontaneous nephew challenged.

Since meeting deadlines is a serious matter to Structured people, much stress in their lives stems from the fear that they might be late. If they can hack it, they prefer to hand in papers and reports early to play it safe, in case an emergency crops up. Also, they bank on free time at the end to play, which rarely materializes.

"Sometimes, we hurry to finish projects and jobs only to discover later that the assignment or order has been cancelled," a Structured group member admitted. "The sPontaneous workers kind of smirk at us when that happens."

Those who prefer a Structured lifestyle divide the day into segments and live faithfully by the clock. They are likely to designate certain days for specific jobs. "We have to force ourselves to be flexible," one Structured individual admitted, "because we allow our schedule and plans to become law. Sometimes our plans and schedules are our worst enemies!"

"I used to really admire people who were organized, but now I realize that they can't help it," a sPontaneous observer teased.

Some Structured people give the impression that being organized is synonymous with being spiritually and emotionally mature, as though they taught themselves to be that way.

A certain degree of self-discipline results from an inner determination to control one's will and inclinations, but many highly disciplined and motivated people take total credit for their preference for organization and structure and getting things done without realizing that it stems mostly from how they were wired at birth.

Time-management speakers and proponents of "setting priorities" decry the sPontaneous / Unstructured lifestyle as though it were inferior or a sign of immaturity. This condescending and false attitude intimidates sPontaneous people who struggle in a Structured nation.

Our Creator didn't goof when he created 50 percent of people to be more Unstructured. He knew that Structured "J" people would need sPontaneous counterparts to balance their tendency for workaholism.

Follow your impulse. The sPontaneous group has been gifted with a play ethic. "Work, it must be fun" is their motto, qualified by "I'll do it later!"

Because they dislike being told what to do themselves, they prefer not to be in charge. Independent and stubborn describe most of them to some degree. The sPontaneous crowd does not like to be boxed in. Planning their day or following a prescribed schedule does not appeal to them.

"I like to do things when I first think of them rather than plan ahead," one sPontaneous individual said to the group. "It ruins half the fun if you have to wait for something to happen," another member continued.

"What you plan to do Friday may not materialize, so you avoid disappointment by not planning. Also, appointments made way ahead may conflict with an opportunity to go the beach," someone else expounded.

Unstructured people are process-oriented rather than completion- or closure-oriented. As long as they are challenged by what they are doing, they will continue. That explains why they prefer short-term, exciting projects.

If jobs or responsibilities do not provide much stimulation, they will begin reluctantly and possibly not finish what they started. But their discipline and commitment far outshine Structured peoples' if they are sufficiently challenged.

"We do not work from lists," one sPontaneous group member reminded the others. "We hate lists, lose lists, and wish our parents had understood that. We prefer to let little jobs pile up into one huge challenge. We'll do a better job cleaning if we are working on a disaster area. Please don't tell us when to begin, just when the job has to be finished," was the consensus.

sPontaneous people excel in emergencies or crises. They think clearly and do their best work when they are under time pressure. In fact, they become Structured in a crisis. That is why they are likely to let things slide until the last minute and then "steam it out"—and even get an "A" on the project.

Since life normally consists of more routine than crisis, unless sPontaneous people have trouble-shooting professions, their best potential will go untapped. In their spare time they may follow emergency vehicles or be involved in a sport or recreation that provides some risk factor, for example, rock climbing.

When one Structured group faulted a sPontaneous group for chronic tardiness, the latter countered with "We're not habitually late because of lack of respect for others, but because we hate to wait for things to begin. Most meetings, for example, are pretty boring to us. We'd rather be outside. The first part of meetings is usually spent getting ready to begin, anyway."

A sPontaneous senior engineering student said, "If I get up early, I get to school late. But if I sleep until the last minute, I get everything done—essential things, that is—and still make it to class on time. Extra time encourages me to piddle away the time reading the paper and playing with my cat."

Since the business world is organized and considers respect for the clock and dependability critical criteria for good workmanship, many sPontaneous people lose good jobs due to their poor punctuality and absenteeism. "We do not have the rigid sense of time that Structured people seem to possess," one group member responded.

"When someone says, 'Meet me at 10,' that doesn't mean exactly at 10 to us, but somewhere around there. We do agree, though, that improving our punctuality and dependability should be one of our chief goals."

What Personality Type Are You?

To determine your personality code letters, use the following guide. Circle your preference in each of the four categories listed below: The four letters indicate your type.

E Extroversion	(Social Preference)	I Introversion
S Sensing	(Information Gathering)	N iNtuitive
T Thinking	(Decision Making)	F Feeling Heart-Logic
J Structured (Judging)	(Lifestyle)	P sPontaneous (Unstructured Perceptive)

Introverts usually know if they are introverted; extroverts are often unsure. The individual profiles in the next chapter will help you establish which one describes you mostly and enable you to solidly identify your favorite four-letter preferences.

Keep in mind that everyone assesses all the preferences at some time in varying degrees and that discovering you are some of all the preferences means that you are normal. This truism comes as a relief to many people.

As you become more familiar with the four type arenas, you'll recognize when you are using a particular preference. That's part of the fun of developing this skill. It's much like learning a second language. Recognizing the use of all the preferences is like breathing: it happens so naturally that you are hardly aware.

But as an added incentive to encourage you to adopt this communication skill, I'm delighted to include testimonials submitted by several clients, family members, and friends—all of whom had access only to the interpretation found in this book. (That's how easy it is to embrace this concept.) These individuals share how MBTI information has positively influenced them in life changes, self-esteem, relationships with friends and family, parenting, working with students, counseling, helping patients, and dealing with seniors.

In addition to the testimonials you'll find unique personal profiles that always amaze receivers. In my experience using the MBTI with hundreds of people, only one profile out of the 16 will appeal to you the most. To describe each personality type, I include: a one- to three-word label, an inventory of individual characteristics, and a list of ways that particular type impacts society in general. Each profile closes with a nugget thumbprint paragraph outlining how a community is benefited by that type.

(I recently ran into a professional educator to whom I had given the MBTI 20 years ago. This person shared, "I keep my profile close at hand and read it often when I need a boost in who I really am as I adjust to a new personal situation.")

After the personal profiles a temperament management section follows to help you use the information wisely, answer usual questions, and provide an in-depth analysis that I predict the iNtuitive readers, especially, will appreciate.

A second theme of this book is comparing people's differences, beauty, talent, and needs to that of flowers. I am intrigued with the unique contributions some flowers have besides beauty and fragrance. All blend together in bouquets, gardens, bird feeders, medicines, etc. We, too, are all placed in significant places with talents and abilities to share in God's garden. It's a delightful and beneficial endeavor to learn to blend who we are with the designs of others.

CHAPTER 2

Uniqueness:
Testimonials, Profiles, Management, and Instincts

Be completely humble and gentle;
be patient, bearing with one another in love.
Ephesians 4:2

As we explore the uniqueness of different personality types, we'll share some real-life testimonials before looking at the 16 personal profiles and ways to manage our various temperaments and how our mind works instinctively as needed.

The testimonials are gifts from satisfied users of the blending miracle of relationships. They appear first to demonstrate how easily the communication skill of understanding personalities transfers to getting along with anyone with whom you spend time—no matter the age, education, or situation. Appreciating and understanding the simple adjustments made with various personalities will make better sense after you claim your personal profile and compare the others.

As you read over the 16 profile possibilities, embrace the one that reflects how you see the world, gather information, make decisions, and feel most comfortable when it comes to work or play. Find the profile that fits just one of your friends or relatives to compare the preferences. Some profiles are fairly close, whereas others are miles apart. The lights will go on!

The tips on temperament management are common-sense reminders for being respectful as you introduce personality (MBTI) talk into your conversation. Some people are not interested in knowing who you are or who they are—or don't want others to know who they are. Many people ease into the type-talk eventually. Give them time to absorb the information.

The tips also consider the order of which each preference is accessed. For example, Intuitives are usually the ones asking questions about the preference order. So, every profile is unique and after you become familiar with all the preferences, you'll understand the worth of this information, especially knowing what preference is used on the world and what preference is saved for privacy. (For instance, as an ENFJ, I use my Feeling Heart-Logic on the world in counseling and speaking, but my Intuitive writing is more difficult and used in privacy.) Understanding the uniqueness of your temperament will help you know how to depend on instinct in various situations.

Testimonials

Following are examples from friends, relatives, and clients of how understanding their personality type boosted their self-esteem and also enabled them to sweeten their relationships. Hopefully, their testimonials will trigger your resolve to take advantage of this simple but powerful tool we know as the Myers-Briggs. (You'll notice that the majority of people who responded to this project prefer the iNtuitive preference!)

INTP and ESFJ Living as Total Opposites

"A fellow counselor was so excited about the information generated by the Myers-Briggs that I asked him if he would let me take the Indicator. When I got my results as an INTP I couldn't believe that described who I am, although the instrument only generated the results from my answers. Close friends affirmed these results; the Myers-Briggs had nailed it (or me).

"I wondered what my wife of 24 years might generate as a personality type. She wasn't interested in taking the questionnaire since she is a very private person and doesn't relish others' knowing that much about her. So, I decided to answer the questions for her. I had known her long enough that I thought I could come up with accurate results. The results showed she is my opposite ESFJ, or as Carl Jung calls it, "my shadow." No wonder what she sees as black, I see as white.

"The revelation this information had for me was that I was trying to manage our marriage by treating her the way I wanted to be treated. I was trying to do unto her as I would have her do unto me. This was the reverse of what I needed to be doing. I needed to recognize that she is different from me and I need to treat her the way her personality wants to be treated and take myself out of the equation. This reversal caused a noticeable improvement in our relationship, which wasn't that bad but it is now much better. She responded to my change in a very positive way.

"This doesn't mean that everything has become peace and harmony, but it does give us a framework by which we can judge ourselves and better understand the behavior of the other. I have used the Myers-Briggs in my counseling practice ever since that year and have enjoyed seeing couples open their eyes to each other with a new appreciation for each other and seeing differences as a challenge to growth rather than obstacles to happiness."

ENFJ and ISTJ Accepting Differences

"Discovering that I'm an ENFJ desiring to solve emotional problems and my mate is an ISTJ, introverted, matter-of-fact Thinker has helped me to be more patient with him. I understand that's it's normal for him to need time to think, so I am more willing to wait for an answer than expecting one right away.

"Also, because he is legitimately not a people person, I see why he leaves church when I'm still conversing with some folks. I have accepted that if I introduce him, he won't say much or initiate a conversation with them. He even says that he doesn't know those people—and he prefers to keep it that way! He will literally back out of a room if he feels uncomfortable. In my personal life he uses his thoughtful actions to communicate his love.

"He doesn't see the value in talking out problems, but will give facts to back up his opinion. I've gotten used to his ISTJ personality and wouldn't want to change him, nor could I."

ENFJ Male Experiencing Life Changes

"I knew nothing about temperament until I met Ruth Ward about 30 years ago. As a matter of fact, I thought I was messed up, always wrong. It seemed my whole life was an apology. I was striving to prove my life had value, but nothing I did was enough.

"At a conference we shared, Ruth introduced me to the MBTI. As she explained the results, and talked with me personally about my circumstances, I experienced, relief, excitement, and freedom. Not only did I learn something in those sessions, but I also began a journey that continues on a daily basis.

"Relationships are hard, but as I learn more about the 16 types, understanding my adult daughters and others becomes easier. Learning that my older brother was a private, facts-oriented Thinker explained why we locked horns. But his artistic INFP wife and I saw eye to eye because our personalities were similar. Being softhearted, we both struggled with hurt feelings around my brother.

"I've learned to respond according to my honest feelings and opinions rather than the way I think others expect, which has given me relief and increased my confidence. And it's helpful to know that it's normal for tenderhearted males to need affirmation and approval from others. My sense of value has increased and contributes to my spiritual growth and relationship with God."

INTJ Female Experiencing Professional Enrichment

"MBTI has been a tool in my ministry toolbox for 30 years. When I took it and then Ruth interpreted it, my life was changed. In fact, it was transformative for me.

"I always had believed and felt that I was in a parallel universe with peers—especially female friends. I never understood why until I began to learn what being an INTJ had to do with it. I owned my preferences and turned them into life strengths.

"I learned my nonpreferences as well as the need to be aware of how they can develop blind spots for me that can be detrimental to my leadership and management.

My career has involved administration and personnel for most of my working years. Applying a working knowledge of MBTI to both has been invaluable, but especially with personnel.

"If you want hilarious stories, those would come from people who have worked under me. They would warn each other how I would receive this or that. Later they would tell me. They were always right—dead on. They knew me well, and I was consistent and transparent.

"Another impact MBTI has had on me is that people from every work setting I have been in choose to keep up with me. They didn't hate me! Much of that is thanks to the mirror held up to me to begin to understand this female INTJ.

"Understanding the idiosyncrasies common to female INTJs has helped me keep a sense of humor about myself and the puzzled look people sometimes have about my behaviors or attitudes. Now, as I approach retirement from my vocation, I enjoy flexing my nonpreferences. I extrovert more and I love being more spontaneous and less structured."

ENFJ and INFJ Seniors Undergoing Profile Switches

"Irene and I still invite guests to our home with joy, but her Introversion has moved to Extroversion and vice-versa for me. She is now the central person who greets and dialogues with all our guests while I prefer to focus on one or two at a time rather than a group as in the past."

"We've made adjustments to provide a comfortable event for all," Irene added. "Adjusting to only one difference in personality still demands lifelong effort with some successes and failures. The bond that holds us together is the vow we took at our wedding. The gradual switching of preferences has been refreshing and enjoyable for both of us."

ENFJ Pastor / Counselor / Professor Applying MBTI

"As a retired pastor who was actively involved in counseling couples, I requested that each take the MBTI for themselves, then again to answer for their intended spouse. Couples were amazed how differently one partner experiences the other from how they understand themselves. It is at the point of differing understandings that new understanding and appreciation surfaces. This of course may lead to long-term reconciliation that involves learning communication skills.

"The MBTI information currently helps me as an adjunct professor in relating positively and helpfully with young and older adult college students."

ENFJ and ENFP Adjusting to One Preference Difference

"We were already in our careers and set in our ways when we set up housekeeping. The personality analysis we took revealed that we gave the exact same answers except for two! Would you rather sky dive or read a book? We differ only in the Lifestyle preference: I'm structured; Ted is spontaneous. We asked the psychologist what this would mean for our life together. He said, 'It may be boring because you'll always know what the other one is thinking!' This variation took some adjustment on both of our parts, but having three preferences in common has also been very helpful.

"Ted has always loved to just dart off to do something totally unplanned and unexpected. On the other hand, I revel in the planning of an experience and seeing it all work out just as expected. This over-thinking and planning each detail whether it be a party or a vacation drove him nuts.

"After a year of marriage, Ted planned a surprise anniversary weekend trip to a cabin in the mountains. 'Pack your bag. We're going to the mountains—NOW! Surprise!' I had appointments; I didn't know if our budget could handle the expense. I freaked out. It was a mind-blowing tizzy for me. But we went and I tried to relax, but the whole time I was fretting over whether all the details were going to work out; they did, but the structured me didn't handle the spontaneity well.

"Thirty-seven years later I planned a two-week road trip to California. I spent months perusing the websites knowing what would interest him. I had charts of all kinds with the vital information listed for reservations, directions, etc.

"We had a marvelous time, and the plans worked out perfectly just as intended. Ted appreciated a well-executed trip where he didn't have to work out the minute details and he got to choose what we'd do once we got to a destination. Skydiving wasn't my choice but definitely appealed to his spontaneity.

"I endeavor to leave plenty of time in my planning to allow for his spontaneity. We are still learning to bend for each other's Structured-Spontaneous tendencies to maintain a happily forever after."

ESFJ Appreciating INTP Mate, Adult INFJ Son, Adult ESTJ Son

"One domestic issue that used to frustrate me was my partner's lack of organization around the house. As a matter of fact, I can remember accusing him of not caring about me, since he would let his clothes, gear, etc. lay around. I know that was wrong, so gradually we agreed to manage our own spaces. He manages his space his way, and I manage mine, well, differently.

"Then, I think about all the ideas, ideas, ideas. He likes the process of coming up with ideas, as does one of our sons. But our other Sensing-Structured son and I just like simple decisive action. We need a little of both in our relationships for sure, and we have come to appreciate each person's ability and draw on it when needed. Unlike me, my husband can always come up with good ideas in an emergency!

"The most difficult difference for me over the years, though, has been the Heart-Logic vs. Head-Logic in temperament. I've had to rely less on feelings and emotion and become much more logical, but I don't think my husband and son will ever move to the middle. My Feeling son and I communicate better, and our Head-Logic son and his dad see eye to eye because of sharing the Thinking preference. It is interesting to me that while I am always most comfortable around people with temperaments like mine, I am drawn to opposites. I've discovered that is because I appreciate new ideas that iNtuitives always have to share."

ENFJ Understanding Sensing-Feeling Friends

"As an iNtuitive I like variety in a lot of areas of life and especially in friendships. I want to be everyone's friend but no one's best friend—or I would feel smothered. I have to be careful with Sensing-Feeling friends who need an exclusive best friend. I am a faithful and supportive friend, but don't want to get caught up in too much daily drama."

ESFJ Encouraging Elderly Parents

"As my parents reached their 90s, they found they had much more time together. On the surface this would look like a good thing, but a lot of togetherness periodically created tension that became my problem to deal with as I listened to each of their complaints.

"My ISTJ mother and my ENFP father were getting on each other's nerves. He would be well intended to accomplish the tasks she had asked him to do, but would get distracted with another little project. He may or may not have gotten back to the original goal.

"I was able to share with Mom that it would be very difficult for Dad to follow a Structured routine, knowing that he was Spontaneous. Mom and I discovered that in the big picture, any particular hands-on job could be delayed without a problem since he was iNtuitive.

"On the other hand, Dad would teasingly call Mom the Little General since she was able to see things that needed to be attended to and, no longer being able to do them herself, created a to-do list and expected this list to be taken care of pronto.

"The Myers-Briggs Indicator provided valuable insight for buffering the resistance my dad felt with her lists by lending my Sensing-Structured helping hand to assist him in completing her lists and simultaneously giving my dad and me, both tenderhearted, quality time together."

ENFJ Professional Meeting Patients' Needs

"As a professional health care worker who worked closely on patients who I would see a number of times a year, I learned to make sure our time together did not violate their personalities. I have a good sense of how people are wired. When working with patients and chatting with them, if I noticed their eyes starting to glaze over, I knew they had heard enough. Or if I knew they were introverts, I wouldn't chatter too much or ask personal questions unless it pertained to their care. However, these same introverts would open up to me after they knew me and trusted me. I loved that. I also wouldn't offer too much detailed information to iNtuitives, as they love the big picture. The Sensing clients preferred hearing the step-by-step details over again."

ENFJ Female Adjusting to Opposite INTP Husband

"The MBTI information has brought so much freedom to my relationships in allowing myself and others to be ourselves. With my INTP husband, I know if he's silent it doesn't mean he's mad at me. It means he wants some quiet time. I endeavor not to plan too many activities close together with many people unless I'm prepared for him to retreat. He doesn't retreat physically anymore but has learned to mentally retreat. Conversely, I will go nuts with days of just puttering and no people interaction, so we jointly strike a balance."

ENFJ Coping with Children's Opposite Preferences

"When my older INTP sPontaneous son was four, I discovered that it worked better if I did not tell him the plans I made but let it all unfold like a surprise. However, my younger INFJ Structured son wanted and needed to know the plans—what day it was and what time it was. Knowing that their differences were normal gave me confidence as a parent."

ENFJ Understanding INTP Head-Logic Husband

"My Thinking iNtuitive husband can make some seemingly harsh statements to me or others, but I have learned that he means well but also that he possesses a different perspective and understands negative situations faster. He sizes people up accurately and quickly. On the other hand, because I'm Feeling I give people way too much space at times. It's good to see the truth when the emotion is taken out of it."

Profiles

When I first learned about the MBTI, I immediately changed from teaching school to counseling full time. I'm very indebted to the MBTI information for providing me with the courage to change my career path. And even though that was 33 years ago, applying the Myers-Briggs to relationships is still a major player in my life.

As I composed each of the following profiles, I kept in mind the persons I know well who represent each four-letter personality type. Each personal profile has four segments that represent two preferences in each:

1. Social: Introvert or Extrovert
2. Information/fact gathering: Sensing or iNtuitve
3. Decision making: Thinking (Head-Logic) or Feeling (Heart-Logic)
4. Lifestyle: Structured (Judging) or Unstructured (sPontaneous)

The description of each personality type includes a personal inventory related to its four letters (preferences), a list of specific character/personality traits for those four preferences, and the impact of that personlity type on his/her community or society. Enjoy finding and claiming your unique profile. In fact, there's only one that will suit you well.

ISFJs: Servers

I = Introversion

_____prefer privacy and quiet, and working alone

_____think before speaking and therefore make few verbal errors

_____tire from spending long periods with people

S = Sensing

_____gather information using the senses

_____dislike changes

_____collect, respect, and remember facts

_____prefer working with hands rather than ideas

_____consider past good decisions when making current decisions

F = Feeling

_____consider other people in making decisions

_____are warm, easily moved, compassionate

_____must have harmony

_____are sensitive to criticism and appreciation

_____can be taken advantage of due to softheartedness

_____seek others' approval before making most decisions

J = Structured

_____prioritize completing projects

_____function better with a schedule and little wasted time

_____like to know what is expected ahead of time

_____have an ethic that work comes before play

ISFJs:

• make up 6% of the population, with males underrepresented
• desire to serve and minister to individual needs
• enjoy keeping up with past events and relationships
• value conservation of money and possessions
• appreciate tradition
• believe work is good and that play must be earned
• are willing to work long hours to complete a task
• have an ethic of "work, it must be done"
• enjoy repetitive chores, doing things the same way and according to the rules
• rarely question an established procedure as long as it is efficient and effective
• are provoked when others violate or ignore standard operating procedures or rules
• turn annoyances inward, sometimes causing fatigue and anxiety
• are super dependable
• are seldom happy working in situations where rules are constantly changing
• work in occupations such as nursing, teaching, clerical, medicine, librarian, middle management administration
• render service gently and helpfully without recognition
• delight in assisting the underdog and handle thankless service well
• have an extraordinary sense of responsibility
• focus on practical concerns rather than speculating about ideas concerning the unknown

ISFJs:

... are down to earth, aware of the value of material resources, abhor wasting or misusing material and resources, prefer to save something for a rainy day, and prepare for emergencies.

... are uncomfortable in positions of authority because they tend to do all the work themselves rather than insisting that others do their part. Consequently, they are frequently overworked.

... are family people, make excellent homemakers and parents, usually are meticulous house and groundskeepers, expect children to conform to rules of the community, dislike putting on airs, like quiet friends rather than boisterous ones, and are often good cooks.

… are frequently misunderstood and undervalued and are easily taken for granted along with their behind-the-scenes contributions, fueling feelings of resentment. That bottled-up emotion can gnaw inwardly, causing much undeserved suffering.

… like to get things done—and done right. They are loyal to institutions and may get impatient with delayed projects due to another's procrastination.

… like to be appreciated for the product they produce. They value caution, carefulness, thoroughness, and accuracy of work. They enjoy hearing comments about what they have produced, especially if a product or service meets the standards set forth. They like to be recognized as responsible, loyal, and industrious but have a hard time showing pleasure when it is given.

ISFJs keep the nation's feet on the ground, serving faithfully and quietly behind the scenes and completing unending service and responsibilities.

ISFPs: Sympathizers

I = Introversion

_____prefer privacy to people

_____enjoy being with only one or two persons at a time

_____prefer working alone

_____think before speaking and therefore make few verbal errors

_____become fatigued when spending time with several people and/or in conversation

S = Sensing

_____are very observant and skillful in picking up common-sense facts

_____enjoy hands-on projects

_____find planning ahead or solving people problems to be difficult

F = Feeling

_____involve people in decision making

_____are sensitive to criticism

_____need approval and appreciation

_____want peace and harmony

_____are happier as a coach rather than a boss

P = sPontaneous

_____are practical and facts-and-figures oriented

_____make decisions at the last minute

_____dislike being bossed

_____handle crises well

ISFPs:
- make up 6% of the population, with males underrepresented
- use sPontaneous hands-on abilities in the community
- are free-spirited and need freedom
- purposely avoid getting too tied to people or work
- usually want excitement and pleasure, but nothing boisterous
- are musical, colorful, warm, alive, sweet, colorful, natural, absolute
- prefer to communicate through action, offering a flower, a smile, a plate of cookies, or a service
- enjoy outdoor activities
- are fun to be with because of a play-ethic that supersedes work
- are attracted to physical crises needs
- enjoy people but prefer a certain detachment
- are fiercely independent and insistent on living for the present
- enjoy quiet excitement
- are loyal friends
- are friends with their children but can become very firm
- are extravagant with gifts and generous with their time and possessions but live simply themselves

ISFPs:

... are down to earth, aware of the value of material resources, abhor wasting or misusing material and resources, prefer to save for a rainy day, and prepare for emergencies.

... are uncomfortable in positions of authority because they tend to do all the work themselves rather than insist that others do their part. Consequently, ISFPs are frequently overworked.

... are family people, make excellent homemakers and parents, usually are meticulous house and grounds keepers, expect children to conform to rules of the community, dislike putting on airs, like quiet friends rather than boisterous ones, and are often good cooks.

... are frequently misunderstood and undervalued. They are easily taken for granted along with their behind-the-scenes contributions, fueling feelings of resentment. The bottled-up emotion can gnaw inwardly, causing much undeserved suffering.

... like to get things done—and right. They are loyal to institutions and may get impatient with delayed projects due to someone's procrastination.

... like to be appreciated for the product they produce. They value caution, carefulness, thoroughness, and accuracy of work. They like to be recognized as responsible, loyal, and industrious. They need approval, but have difficulty showing pleasure when it is given.

ISFPs tolerate discomfort, deprivation, hunger, fatigue, and pain and show courage quietly without asking for praise. They continue working, playing, and practicing often beyond reasonable limits for other types but dislike being told what to do. Their friends, family, and co-workers appreciate their unselfish behind-the-scenes caregiving.

ISTJs: Conscientious Workers

I = Introversion

_____prefer privacy to people

_____think before speaking and then clearly state what's intended, resulting in few verbal errors

_____become exhausted after being around people for long periods

_____need recuperation after a day's work and/or extroverting

S = Sensing

_____respect logical, obvious common-sense, researched facts

_____prefer working with hands more than with ideas

_____accept routine as long as it has meaning

T = Thinking

_____make solid, consistent decisions based on known, accurate facts

_____are skilled in looking at things impersonally

J = Structured

_____enjoy planned days and knowing expectations

_____are defined by an ethic of "Work, it must be done"

ISTJs:

• make up 6% of the population, with females underrepresented

• are dependable and dutiful

• are decisive in practical affairs

• are loyal to institutions, organizations, and traditions

- are faithful to one's word
- are quiet and serious at home and work
- hate to waste time, money, or effort
- enjoy mending, fixing, and saving
- work without drawing attention to self
- receive little notice or appreciation for their work
- are attracted to details
- do not take chances with money
- are sometimes seen as cold and distant in decision making
- make decisions based on solid, reasonable facts
- stick to decisions and are not intimidated by persons who disagree
- want social events to proceed in a pre-planned, orderly, pleasant manner
- accept time and resource demands from others if requests are sensible
- seldom complain of boredom
- are content to live on an even keel
- enjoy routine and do not like a lot of change
- resent having to meet another's agenda when away from work
- will not quit work on a task unless experience proves otherwise
- make decisions based on cause and effect without considering other people first
- give self-approval but want respect and trust from others

ISTJs:

 … have a strong desire to be trusted. They reflect a sober and careful character.

 … want to be useful and helpful. They want things done orderly and efficiently. They are attracted to hands-on jobs that involve a desire to conserve such as teaching, banking, auditing, accounting, clerking, medicine, insurance, managing, and selling.

 … are sometimes so eager to serve that they have difficulty refusing added responsibility, worried about who will do it if they don't.

 … are the stabilizers of the social and economic world. They believe in a good day's work for a good day's pay and cannot understand anyone who shirks responsibility.

 … have difficulty understanding the emotional needs of Feeling types. They can be sarcastic and critical but forget their hurtful words very quickly and expect others to also.

 The role of ISTJs in the business of the world is extremely important. Their accuracy and staying firm in Head-Logic decision making keep their community balanced.

ISTPs: Unstoppable Operators

I = Introversion

_____prefer quiet and privacy more than people

_____think before speaking and then clearly state what's intended, resulting in few verbal errors

_____find long periods with people to be exhausting

S = Sensing

_____are good at gathering facts from logical, obvious sources

_____keep good track of facts and rely on them in making decisions

_____enjoy the routine of doing same action-oriented tasks

T = Thinking

_____make decisions without regard to what others say

_____stick with decisions unless someone close brings to mind an important emotional consideration

P = sPontaneous

_____prefer a non-structured day and play over work

_____dislike receiving or giving orders

ISTPs:
- make up 6% of the population, with females underrepresented
- give tireless attention and concentration to chosen activities
- gravitate toward careers such as first responders, performing artists, craft artisans, and technicians/scientists
- do not enjoy service and clerical work
- procrastinate when doing boring and/or lifestyle jobs
- can be unpredictable, impulsive, and/or restless
- are impatient with slow activities such as sitting, reading, and idle chatter
- can become grouchy, anxious, and moody in the absence of activity
- are capable of giving self-approval, but want respect and trust from others

ISTPs:

...enjoy being involved in an activity or project but not necessarily to finish. The actual process of involvement is intriguing. Activity is an end in itself.

... enjoy quietness and solitude and activities where body movement is involved more than face-to-face dialogue—for example, mountain climbing, hunting, fishing, and sports, etc., and/or can be distant and detached for this reason.

... prefer the use of knowledge rather than accumulating knowledge. Advanced education interests them only so far as it helps them gain expertise in a particular activity or project. They prefer experience, action, and on-the-job learning.

… are sports people—spectator or participant or both. Probably 50% of surfers are ISTPs, for surfing requires a willingness to perfect performance and concentration and to tolerate solitude and risk.

… respond to the challenge of complicated equipment that provides action. For example, large trucks, earth movers, and construction machinery fascinate ISTPs. They also find their need for excitement and action met in such occupations as surgery, electronics, car racing, bicycle racing, dare-devil acts, acrobatics, and athletics.

…tend to be outstanding craftsmen such as sculptors, wood carvers, furniture and cabinet makers, weavers, and rug makers.

ISTPs are appreciated for quietly performed hands-on skills and rescues that receive little recognition. Some people regard them as snobbish or dull because friendships materialize only after getting to know someone well. Communities celebrate their generosity of time and expertise.

ESFJs: Hosts and Hostesses

E = Extroversion
> _____need a lot of people and little privacy
> _____talk while thinking, requiring erasure of statements often
> _____are motivated by interaction with people

S = Sensing
> _____focus on gathering, remembering, trusting, and repeating facts that ensue from experiences with the senses
> _____learn through experience and rarely repeat a mistake

F = Feeling
> _____check with others before making a decision
> _____find unemotional decisions tough
> _____need praise and affirmation

J = Structured
> _____plan daily activities and follow the schedule
> _____want to know expectations before making plans

ESFJs:
- make up 13% of the population, with males underrepresented
- are very sociable and talkative
- make outstanding hosts and hostesses
- find importance in social and family ties and traditions

• enjoy reminiscing over old stories
• desire to be appreciated both for themselves and for their services
• are hurt by indifference
• take the opinions of others seriously and seek approval of words and actions
• share personal opinions whether invited to or not
• tend to monopolize conversations
• want physical problems settled efficiently and quickly
• function best with schedule and routine
• are faithful mates
• are sympathetic to others

ESFJs:

... are generally quite loquacious, but in a setting of strangers may feel awkward and become quiet. As long as they have facts in common with someone, they can converse indefinitely. They enjoy rehearsing events and facts—blow by blow.

... are outgoing but wear their heart on their sleeves. They yearn to be needed, loved, and appreciated and are apt to become melancholy if they are blamed for people problems.

... are extremely sentimental, inspiring them to plan and finance parties commemorating special days and to enjoy organizing social events.

... enjoy the process of decision making, especially when the focus is on the welfare of others.

... are drawn to service careers and occupations such as selling, social work, coaching, teaching, supervision, and food and health services.

ESFJs are known by their generous gifts of time and money spent keeping in touch with family and friends, planning parties, organizing photos, and helping with the clean-up after get-togethers. They are never too busy to help anyone, and keep every visitor comfortable. Communities love and appreciate this type.

ESFPs: Performers

E = Extroversion
_____are motivated by being with people
_____talk before listening, resulting in verbal errors
_____are naturally confident and optimistic

S = Sensing

_____draw facts from senses of hearing, smelling, seeing, touching, and tasting

_____remember, respect, rely on, and trust facts

_____enjoy hands-on projects, shopping, planning parties, and running errands

F = Feeling

_____make emotional decisions based on people rather than just cause and effect

_____are open to changing their mind when someone's needs, demands, or wishes become apparent

_____display warmth and generosity that come from emotional decision making

P = sPontaneous

_____prefer unplanned days

_____dislike authority

_____possess a play ethic

_____prefer doing work at will rather than on a prescribed schedule

_____tend to be starters but not finishers

ESFPs:

- make up 13% of the population, with males underrepresented
- radiate attractive warmth and optimism
- are talkative, witty, charming, clever, and all-inclusive
- are generous and fun or entertaining to be with
- do not enjoy being alone
- find being with people pleasurable and easy
- have a contagious joy of living
- make outstanding conversationalists
- enjoy the good things in life—dress, food, physical comfort, happy times, new fashion, etc.
- love parties and exist in a continual party-like atmosphere
- are always ready for company, excitement, and fun

ESFPs:

... make exciting, if somewhat unpredictable, mates and parents—which may give quieter types some anxiety and tension from living on the edge of adventure.

... can be generous to a fault. They want to help everyone without return of the favor. They love freely without expecting something in return.

... have a talent for enjoying life and being in the center of conversation, jokes, and fun. They love to go to parties but may leave before time to clean up.

… as parents will be entertaining, friendly, and sources of fun and excitement. When sickness or trouble surfaces, however, they have a low tolerance and may become impatient and desire to leave until the situation improves.

… prefer active jobs and should not be given lonely, solitary assignments. They have outstanding public relations skills. They make decisions with personal and genuine warmth.

… rely heavily on their personal experiences and generally show good common sense. They can be counted on to have accurate data about the people around them, gaining information through effortless and continuous observations through their eyes and ears.

… are not deeply interested in scholastic pursuits because they want knowledge only for immediate utility. They generally avoid careers in science and engineering and instead move toward business, social services involving child and elder care, coaching, foods, retail, medical fields, and fitness and exercise.

ESFPs stand out for chatter and humorous recounting of events. They are admired for their love of family and unselfish reaching out in physical crises and times of need.

ESTJs: Organizers

E = Extroversion

_____enjoy social contact

_____speak extemporaneously and easily

_____are not deterred by verbal errors

_____exude confidence

S = Sensing

_____adhere to logical facts from the environment

_____trust their senses more than facts

_____are intrigued by facts and figures

_____are skilled at working with their hands

T = Thinking

_____make decisions based on what can be seen or proven

_____are not swayed by peoples' wants, expectations, or demands

_____stick to their opinions and decisions unless persuaded otherwise by a significant other person

_____desire personal judgment to be trusted

J = Structured

_____gain stability through structure and routine and a planned day

_____achieve purpose in serving by leadership and being needed

_____find finishing new physical or repair projects never boring

_____contribute through decisiveness

ESTJs:
- make up 13% of the population, with females underrepresented
- are in touch with the external environment
- are pillars of strength, responsible, and dutiful
- are outstanding at organizing orderly procedures and in detailing rules and regulations
- work without needing recognition
- like to see things done correctly
- tend to be impatient with people who do not carry out logical procedures with attention to details and/or authority
- are comfortable evaluating others
- tend to judge how a person is doing in terms of standard operating procedures
- are realistic and matter-of-fact
- enjoy history and following all kinds of sports
- are loyal to institutions and organizations
- make excellent managers, employees, mates, and parents
- give self-approval but want respect and trust from others

ESTJs:

… enjoy seeing friends, former colleagues, and relatives and are relatively easy to get to know. They do not tend to confuse people by sending double messages. They are dependable and consistent, and what they seem to be is what they are.

… are not always responsive to the points of view and emotions of others and may have a tendency to jump to conclusions too quickly. They may not always be willing to listen patiently to opposing views and are especially vulnerable to this tendency when in positions of authority.

… may need to make special effort to remain open to input from others who are dependent on them, for example, their partner, children, and employees.

… like to serve. They are builders / mechanics / maintainers, keeping others socially and economically secure. They are savers and conservators. They strive for everyone to be cared for.

… are protective and logical, and can make decisions and stick to them no matter who or what comes up. Often, they are accused of being "icy" because of their impersonal decisions. "Don't ask questions, just do what I say" describes their personal confidence.

… value hard work with their ethic being, "Work, it must be done." Play comes after work. When finished, they are proud of the product and the standard it meets. They can work with or without harmony and give themselves approval when a project is completed.

… see where their duty lies and are not likely to shirk responsibility, even when this requires considerable sacrifice on their part. They frequently rise to responsible positions in their career and/or religious affiliations. They are punctual, and expect others to be also.

… can be highly influential with their administrative ability. They are often outspoken and ready to voice their opinions. They hunger for accurate facts and figures.

The ability of ESTJs for construction and repairs requires lots of tools for helping anyone with mechanical troubles. Work is their play. They never tire of assisting or directing others. Communities depend on them and gratefully identify them as the "Rock of Gibraltar."

ESTPs: Rescuers

E = Extroversion

_____emanate self-confidence and optimism

_____enjoy retelling events

_____are motivated by association with people

S = Sensing

_____gather and respect facts and figures, using them to protect and rescue people and organizations

_____need physical excitement and action

T = Thinking

_____make shrewd and often impersonal decisions, based on physical facts

_____are rarely taken advantage of

P = sPontaneous

_____find an organized and planned day to be dull

_____follow the idea that "work, it must be fun"

_____can complete tasks at the last minute

_____dislike anyone giving orders

ESTPs:
- make up 13% of the population, with females underrepresented
- enjoy action and inspire action
- view life as a game
- are resourceful and popular
- love people but can be possessive of them, especially family
- like to be in charge and have their orders respected
- give self-approval but desire respect and trust from others

ESTPs:

... live up to their name: rescuers. Many are drawn to first responder roles such as firefighters and law enforcement. Others are physicians, builders, athletes, etc. They are gifted in keeping their cool.

... prefer working or playing outdoors. They can be found on road work operating heavy machinery such as cranes and backhoes and working in dangerous situations.

... know how to save money, time, and effort. Risk does not threaten them—only challenges. Never daunted in their efforts, they are several steps ahead in anticipated outcomes.

... often feel that the end justifies any means. They have extraordinary talent for pulling businesses, institutions, and households out of financial or administrative difficulty. However, they dislike the tedious paperwork of wrapping up a project.

... are dependent on structured helpers who handle intricate details to ensure success.

... want every moment to be brimming with excitement and action. They'll invest their total personalities in recounting endless tales and clever jokes embellished with charisma.

... read people quickly, picking up non-verbal clues that enable them to be shrewd salespersons and persuasive conversationalists.

... are apt to control conversations, possessing the ability to aim remarks like an arrow or sharp dagger. They have a knack for finding what will work.

ESTPs never seem to tire of initiating games and fun and of quickly handling physical emergencies, giving orders without hesitation. Communities are indebted to their confidence and courage in handling disasters.

INFJs: Empathizers

I = Introversion

_____prefer the world of privacy and quietness

_____speak only after thinking, then say what's intended and make few verbal errors

_____need recuperation after being with people for an extended time

N = iNtuitive

_____prefer the world of ideas

_____are distracted from routine responsibilities by the pursuit of abstract goals and ideas

_____create games to make boring jobs fun and to help time pass

F = Feeling

_____make decisions based primarily on feelings, focusing on keeping peace and harmony

_____easily take blame for people problems

J = Structured

_____prefer an organized and planned day with clear expectations

_____believe that work must be done before play

_____are able to see what needs to be done and who should do it

INFJs:
- make up 1% of the population, with males underrepresented
- have an unusual committed drive to contribute to the welfare of others
- are understood only by those very close
- embrace many undisclosed goals
- have many reasons for decisions
- intrigue and entertain others with a vivid imagination
- find understanding of self to be puzzling at times

INFJs:

... are sensitive, quiet, and serious and tend to be perfectionists—often working too hard on a project. They have to improve on whatever they're doing.

... like to be appreciated for their creative ideas, thoughtful gifts, and personal concern. They are surprised to learn that many people are intimidated by them.

... are usually very cooperative because they are organized and crave harmony at all costs. Their spirits are crushed by criticism. They do not want their failures mentioned.

... insist on maintaining a good reputation, which is most important to them.

... are usually good students who use their creativity to achieve significant benefits for others, especially in fighting for a cause.

… must be involved with people, but on a one-on-one basis, working in therapy, counseling, music, art, painting, clinical psychology, medicine, psychiatry, psychology, ministry, writing, or research or teaching in these fields.

… succeed in their chosen fields because of their warmth and genuine concern mixed with enthusiasm, insight, concentration, and ability to complete tasks.

… had rather make suggestions than decisions. They wield much behind-the-scenes influence and are known for stating their strong opinions to their family and friends.

The family and acquaintances of INFJs are often unaware of their behind-the-scenes gifts of creativity, suggestions, time, energy, and finances in assisting those who need help and encouragement. The community is enriched by their gentle, unpresumptuous ways that deserve to be acknowledged and celebrated.

INFPs: Idealists

I = Introversion

_____need much privacy and just a few people

_____speak only after thinking

_____are exhausted after being around people for long periods

_____want quietness in the morning

N = iNtuitive

_____focus on ideas rather than facts and figures

_____are prone to wonder and consider the "what ifs"

_____have many questions but lack confidence to verbalize them

_____disregard facts seen as having no importance

_____gather only a few facts before making impulsive decisions

_____often speak in sentence fragments

_____are highly imaginative

F = Feeling

_____involve others in personal actions, work, and decisions

_____are easily influenced with another's idea if it will maintain harmony or help someone

_____find that making Head-Logic decisions and sticking to them is difficult

P = sPontaneous

_____let things slide until a bit of a crisis requires actions

_____are very flexible and fun to watch

_____despise routine but can spend long hours doing something of personal interest

_____like to start things but have trouble finishing due to loss of interest
_____desire freedom in choosing activities and schedules

INFPs:
• make up 1% of the population, with males underrepresented
• are intellectually profound because ideas are free from structure
• are gifted in learning and working with various languages
• are sensitive, modest, and analytical
• are very dedicated to chosen causes but despair when pursuits fail
• quietly and effectively campaign for individual concerns but can be outspoken when rebuke is needed
• desire unity
• may experience negativity, expecting emotional problems
• are moody and difficult to understand
• avoid visibility, so the ability to problem-solve is often overlooked
• have several goals and many reasons for decisions
• may invent plausible explanations for acts or opinions that are actually based on other causes
• are free-spirited and fiercely resist being put in a box or on a schedule
• often forget things or lose items
• dislike cleaning house or other mundane chores but will do these well for others
• are sensitive and can be taken advantage of
• will display a strong personality if pushed to violate their morals, beliefs, or chosen causes

INFPs:
... are attracted to individual crises and are unstoppable in their commitment to personal involvement. They sacrifice physically, financially, and emotionally—often beyond their own strength and reason. Maintaining good reputations are extremely important to them.

... read people very quickly and may perceive one's attitudes before even he or she can. They relate well to most people but at a safe distance.

...dislike interruptions and work well alone. They handle complicated situations but are impatient with routine and meaningless detail. They rarely make errors involving values.

... are drawn to careers involving helping people one on one such as missionary or humanitarian work, college teaching, psychiatry, medicine, art, architecture, psychology, music, etc.

... do not enjoy business and/or bookkeeping, but can do this type of work if the need arises. They prefer unique professions where jobs are tailor-made for them without schedules.

... are reserved about displaying physical affection, although they want to know they are loved, appreciated, admired, and thought about.

... are mostly female, so homemaking naturally falls to their lot. They are challenged by the emotional, spiritual, ethical, nutritional, and social training of children. INFP males struggle to find a satisfying occupation.

... sometimes become discouraged because they have a tendency to see what won't work in dealing with personalities. They want to succeed but because they are unstructured and dislike hands-on projects, they see little evidence of their accomplishments.

INFPs present an intriguing personality as their ideas of ways to help people unfold. The community desperately needs and appreciates their profound observations, insightful influence, "follower" attitude, and encouragement.

INTJs: Expert Strategists

I = Introversion

_____prefer privacy to people

_____speak only after thinking and then state intentions clearly

_____need recuperation after spending long periods with people

N = iNtuitive

_____are goal-oriented

_____prefer information gathering through ideas, possibilities, and analyses

_____are challenged by theoretical and technical developments

_____always seek to improve over previous accomplishments

T = Thinking

_____make impersonal, calculated decisions based on systematic logic rather than on feeling or emotions

_____can be seen as manipulative

_____stick to decisions even when accused of being coldhearted, uncaring, or selfish

J = Structure

_____are organized and able to complete tasks

_____believe that work must be finished before play time

_____think of work as play

INTJs:
- make up 1% of the population, with females underrepresented
- are gifted in concentrating on possibilities and analyses
- make situation-based logical decisions with little regard for skeptics
- are entrepreneurs of all kinds, and many choose architecture careers
- deplore wasting time, energy, money, ability, or supplies
- must always improve over yesterday's accomplishments, being in competition with themselves
- are perfectionists and demand much of themselves
- can juggle several unrelated goals at a time
- delight in theory and brainstorming
- can sum up given facts and possibilities brilliantly, completely, and quickly
- have strong reasoning intelligence (which males can find challenging in females)
- have difficulty in teen years meeting people like themselves but find more connections in college
- usually complete higher educational goals and may become presidents or CEOs of organizations
- give self-approval but expect respect and trust from others

INTJs:

... are filled with abstract ideas and deadlines, often presenting an unemotional, cold, sober, and all-business attitude—even toward family and friends.

... can be very single-minded, which is most often a strength but at other times becomes a weakness. Maintaining a good reputation is extremely important to them.

... take goals of an institution seriously and continually strive to respond to these goals.

... are loyal to the system rather than to individuals within the system.

... think by subtopics, assuming listeners/students know the insignificant details.

... balance their lives by purposely adding hands-on projects to their schedules such as yard work, painting, cooking, music, and physical conditioning.

... are comfortable with the world of computers, which offers the kind of entertainment and challenge for which they yearn.

... can relax while directing others to take care of mundane duties.

Few people can conceive the depths of the brilliance and ability of INTJs. Co-workers and/or family members may question why they do the physical work while INTJs get paid for their ideas. INTJs provide well thought-out concepts and know-how in high technology and management. The community stands in awe of their gifts.

INTPs: Think-Tank Experts

I = Introversion

_____prefer privacy to people

_____speak only after thinking and then state intentions clearly

_____are exhausted after spending long periods with people

N = iNtuitive

_____gather information through ideas, design, and possibilities

_____find theoretical and technical developments challenging

_____always seek to improve over previous accomplishments

_____place more value on recognition for ideas and design than in monetary gain

T = Thinking

_____make decisions based on logic more than on feelings or emotions

_____stick to decisions unless persuaded otherwise by someone close

_____are not accustomed to expressing appreciation for others and their efforts

P = sPontaneous

_____deal with the world through thoughts and ideas

_____may let responsibilities slide if considered unimportant or boring

_____want every endeavor to be enjoyable

_____have difficulty investing time and effort in less enjoyable causes

INTPs:
- make up 1% of the population, with females underrepresented
- focus on ideas under construction
- strive to be exact and original at the same time
- have sophisticated concentration ability and respect for intelligence
- are sometimes seen as arrogant and intimidating
- are attracted to careers in engineering involving blueprints, research, computers, music, and higher education
- relish the freedom, freshness, and privacy of the outdoors
- can't resist challenges and seeking to understand something complex
- are ready to leave a technique after mastering it
- have varied goals and many reasons for decisions
- may invent plausible explanations for acts or opinions that are actually based on other causes
- give self-approval but desire respect and trust from others

INTPs:

… are often totally unaware of the individual needs and feelings of others and are difficult to understand because they live and move in the impersonal analytical and logical world.

… prefer to think up solutions or designs rather than carry out the routine details of physical creation. Consequently, the finishers often receive the credit for INTPs' work.

… focus on theory and brainstorming. Maintaining a good reputation is extremely important to them.

… often present an unemotional, sober, and even uncaring, attitude toward family and friends because their minds are always swirling with abstract ideas.

… may not emerge from the "lab" for 36 hours when they get involved in a project because their time is not measured by hours. They may even redesign the sequence of time to suit their personal needs.

… may present a disheveled look in their appearance, desks, and personal possessions, but they know where important papers are. They are more concerned about design.

INTPs provide their community with gifts of unusual design, creative ideas, and analyses. Because they do not draw attention to themselves, however, they will possibly feel like aliens until their family, friends, and co-workers gain an understanding of and appreciation for their unique behind-the-scenes gifting.

ENFJs: Encouragers

E = Extroversion

_____appreciate privacy but can handle many people relationships

_____think while speaking

_____are naturally bent toward extemporaneous speaking

_____are optimistic at home and work

N = iNtuitive

_____prefer ideas, theories, goals, and design

_____dislike mundane routine or repetitive action

_____are interested in many subjects but a master of none

_____seek improvement

F = Feeling

_____involve people in making decisions

_____are sensitive to criticism

_____cannot work without peace and harmony

_____function better with approval

_____are easily persuaded by others' needs, wishes, demands, and desires

J = Structured

_____prioritize planning, organization, and finishing projects

_____are adept at delegating

_____are time-conscious but can become sidetracked due to mental involvements

_____follow an ethic of work above all

ENFS:

• make up 5% of the population, with males underrepresented
• enjoy helping others find solutions to life and improve relationships
• patiently donate hours listening and offering tactful suggestions
• are natural counselors, teachers, speakers, writers
• are capable of relating to and drawing out any personality
• shoulder several goals and have many reasons for decisions made
• relate to others with unusual empathy, identifying with the emotions, problems, and beliefs of others
• are easily overextended emotionally
• can depend on hunches, reading other people with accuracy
• have unusual charisma
• are willing to cooperate, and place a high value on cooperation from others
• are good at organizing and keeping track of dates, events, and duties—with the help of detailed lists

ENFJs:

... detest negativism so radically that, as they identify drawbacks, they come across as critical and intimidating to listeners. They attempt to identify ideas they suspect won't work.

... are socially adept and make excellent companions and parents. However, because they are idealists, they want themselves, their marriage, and their family to be perfect.

... want to have a goal or many goals. Without goals, ENFJs become despondent. However, they are interested in so many things, they may have difficulty choosing a career.

… possess a remarkable fluency with conversation, so are good with face-to-face dialogue. Endeavoring to speak one idea at a time in complete sentences is a worthy personal goal.

… are generally surprised but pleased to learn that they exert much influence in committees, on the job, and with their mate, family, neighbors, etc. Reputation is of highest concern.

… love learning and never seem to get enough. They always have dozens of ideas along with scads of questions. They fear boredom.

… prefer to be in charge of their schedules and are often slave drivers of themselves. They are also good at delegating with great diplomacy. They dislike for anyone to waste time.

… find keeping financial records, handling boring physical detail, or wasting time on meaningless pursuits their least favored responsibilities.

ENFJs serve their community with their gifts as influencers, peacemakers, adjusters, encouragers, coaches, teachers, delegators, and speakers.

ENFPs: Catalysts

E = Extroversion

_____prefer people more than privacy

_____tend to combine speaking, listening, and correcting verbal errors

_____are energized by communication

_____bring people together

N = iNtuitive

_____experience spirals of idea spurts

_____find decision making difficult

_____consider possibilities when seeking to solve people's difficulties

F = Feeling

_____consider the welfare of others when making decisions

_____are sensitive to criticism

_____need appreciation, praise, and approval

_____strive for harmony at any cost

_____will take blame unjustly at times to keep peace

P = sPontaneous

_____believe work should be fun

_____tend to let projects slide until the last minute

_____are inspired by pressure to act

ENFPs:
- make up 5% of the population, with males underrepresented
- are full of enthusiastic ideas and good intentions, though not driven to finishing
- seldom carry out creative ideas
- love the process of helping people with any problem
- are attracted to music, writing, creative design, and coaching
- are always willing to answer someone's distress call
- make everything fun
- excel in hospitality and generously open their homes for parties, meetings, and overnight visits
- need to have several goals
- have many reasons for decisions
- sometimes allow friends to drain mental, physical, and financial strength
- work well on solving an emergency relationship or emotional problem
- move from one involvement to the other, always with friends watching, following, and admiring

ENFPs:

... gather information from the unknown, between the lines, and from out of nowhere or hunches.

... love learning and never receive enough. They thrive on discussion. After tasting a new experience, they may move on to another even if the first is not finished.

... prefer the intangible and abstract and are talented in solving emergency problems.

... do not go to bed by the clock, so they are likely to experience poor sleeping and work habits because they enjoy talking all night, not wanting to miss a thing.

... are easily lured away from study, appointments, and routine chores by the promise of exciting dialogue or coming to someone's aid.

... thrive on excitement and action. They find ways around any rule, contending that it's exciting to find one tiny loophole.

... dislike being tied down to a schedule, preferring to be free to assist others.

... need freedom, so having short-term projects suits them

ENFPs are thought by some people to be indispensable because of their ability to quickly address and solve physical and emotional crises. They are fun to be with as they dramatically expound the details of personal experiences. ENFPs work hard to make sure everyone has fun, and in turn, people around them want ENFPs to enjoy who they are.

ENTJs: Head Chiefs

E = Extroversion

_____need some privacy but can handle many people relationships

_____easily verbalize thoughts and speak extemporaneously

_____are optimistic and self-confident

N = iNtuitive

_____need to have several goals simultaneously

_____love theories

_____dislike mundane routine or repetitive action

_____are concerned about reputation

_____thrive on learning, embracing and discussing new ideas, and answering questions

T = Thinking

_____make decisions based on systematic Head-Logic more quickly than on feeling or emotions

_____are sometimes thought to be cold and uncaring due to making impersonal cause-and-effect decisions

J = Structured

_____gain stability through structure and routine and a planned day

_____find challenge in serving by leadership via teaching, advising, and planning the future

_____achieve purpose in finishing analytical, writing, and speaking opportunities

_____contribute by planning, making decisions, and organizing for groups

ENTJs:

• make up 5% of the population, with females underrepresented

• are best known for structured vision

• see a wide range of possibilities

• have a basic need and ability to lead or be in charge

• need to have several goals

• want perfection in everything, including family

• serve as lawyers, physicians, professors, writers, analysts, CEOs, financiers, politicians, heads of organizations, etc.

• sometimes have unrealistic work expectations of self and others

• exude positive authority, reveling in directing subordinates or family members to complete tasks

• feel successful when maintaining a responsible reputation and respect rather than possessions

• give self-approval, but want respect and trust from others

ENTJs:

... consider inefficiency and error in themselves and others intolerable. They respond positively to reminders of the emotional needs of students, fellow workers, family, and friends.

... as administrators, organize their units into a smooth functioning system, planning in advance and keeping both short-term and long-range objectives in mind.

... seek and can see efficiency and effectiveness in personnel. They prefer that decisions be based on impersonal data. They want to work from well-thought-out plans, and like to use engineered operations. They prefer that others follow suit.

... will support the policy of the organization and expect others to do so.

... without realizing it, may come on strong to quieter types and may intimidate others. They are needed to keep people directed and on target, so may feel relaxed and confident in directing others to take care of mundane duties.

... need to avoid coming across as hardnosed and uncaring by reminding themselves that others are entitled to an opinion and that individuality will ease many tense situations.

ENTJs exude intelligence, confidence, and leadership. People feel safe and secure in their presence and under their direction.

ENTPs: Powerful People Movers

E = Extroversion

_____are energized by people involvement

_____can talk and listen at the same time and are not disturbed by verbal errors

_____are self-confident, courageous, and optimistic

N = iNtuitive

_____gather information through ideas, design, and possibilities

_____are challenged by people's need for direction in solving relationship problems

_____are equipped for troubleshooting in the area of personnel

_____tend to overload people with ideas

_____prefer recognition for ideas more than monetary gain

_____value a good reputation

T = Thinking

_____make decisions based on systematic logic more than on feeling or emotions

_____stick to decisions until someone close or new facts persuade otherwise

P = sPontaneous

_____prefer ideas over finished projects

_____tend to let slide responsibilities considered unimportant or boring

_____resist investing time in repetitive or meaningless activities

ENTPs:
- make up 5% of the population, with females underrepresented
- are innovative and enthusiastically interested in everything—the more complex the better
- accept seemingly impossible challenges head-on with excitement and competence
- enjoy risks and the unexpected
- handle emotional crisis problems with calmness and expertise
- relish a people-related challenge that requires creative analysis
- prefer to design and set in motion programs to solve problems rather than being involved in repetitive conversations
- make good entrepreneurs who organize and operate businesses while taking on financial risks
- need to have several goals and many reasons for decisions
- invent plausible explanations for acts or opinions that are actually based on other causes
- give self-approval but want trust and respect from others

ENTPs:

... are some of the most fascinating and witty conversationalists and will often be the center of attention as they engage in and direct their much-loved discussions.

... are likely to transmit an air of arrogance because of their optimistic competence, but they can learn to make people who feel inferior more at ease.

... have an attitude that conveys they know what's going on, which offers security to the more fearful crowd.

... can succeed in many occupations, as long as the job does not involve too much humdrum routine, which makes them restless. They dislike filling out reports.

... are drawn to one or more careers related to writing, speaking, management, counseling, law, construction, firefighting, the military, law enforcement, medicine, politics, and other ventures that require imagination and hard work to meet unusual needs and wants.

... must be challenged or they lose interest and don't follow through.

... are natural people-engineers. Their good humor and optimistic outlook tend to be contagious, and people seek out their company

... are not inspired by orderliness in daily living routines.

ENTPs make entrepreneurial contributions through their humor, innovation, relaxed nature, problem-solving ability in emotional and physical crises, and knack for satisfying everyone.

Temperament Management

Temperament does not label or limit us, but rather frees us to be who we were designed to be. Discovering their personality type completely changes some peoples' view of themselves and others, improving their self-esteem and giving them a new lease on life.

Others who have not struggled with low self-worth, having never been put in a box, just appreciate knowing the legitimate differences in people, and endeavor to make a few immediate adjustments.

Personality typing does not determine attitudes. Two people sharing exactly the same four personality preferences may exhibit very different dispositions, especially if one is female and the other male. Our background in home, school, medical problems, and life experiences contributes greatly to who we are as individuals and how we choose to use our innate gifting.

Everyone wears personality type preferences differently. I like to compare personalities to musical chords in various keys—distinctive in their own right, but enhanced when blended with tones from other keys. The more skilled the musician, the more beautiful the melody. Occasionally people will use their personality type to excuse inappropriate or tactless behavior, for example:

- "Don't fault me for giving you the silent treatment; I'm an introvert."
- "You know how extroverts are; we can't help but ask personal questions."
- "I've always done it this way, and that's the way Sensing people are."
- "I have every right to do this job differently each time because I'm an iNtuitive."
- "It's very normal for Feeling people to get upset, so treat me very gently."
- "Thinkers don't have to say 'I'm wrong' or 'I'm sorry.' You should know by now."
- "I may come across bossy, but that's how Structured people are."
- "I'm late, but it's OK: I'm sPontaneous."

Personality typing is a wonderful tool, but is not to be used as a hammer to beat someone over the head. Some people dislike being analyzed, categorized, or discussed. Respect their privacy. Each of us is like a house with many rooms: we act and respond a little differently depending on which room we're in, with whom, and under what circumstances. We are a blend of:

- reserved / cautious = Introversion (I)
- outgoing / confident = Extroversion (E)
- fact and figure / hands-on = Sensing (S)
- ideas and possibilities = iNtuitive (N)
- organized / closure = Structure (J)
- open-ended / crises = sPontaneous (P)

The Instinctive Working of the Mind

As we encounter the events of a day, we unconsciously shift back and forth between gathering and deciding, meandering from facts and figures (S) and ideas and possibilities (N) to Heart-Logic (F) or Head-Logic (T). Each personality type operates on a specific cycle of the same four preferences common to all types for which each has an inborn comfort-cycle for use. For instance, as an ENFJ, as an event unfolds, here are the steps in my typical "cycle":

1. Contemplate how it will affect others (Heart Logic F).
2. Ponder the possibilities (N).
3. Consider hands-on repetitive facts (S).
4. Call on Head-Logic (T)
[which usually produces guilt when others are hurt or disappointed].

However, I have learned the protective value of accessing Head-Logic and how to identify and nullify the intrusive false guilt. I remind myself often that when Feeling types feel a little bit mean and selfish, they're about right. (False guilt, so common to these types, is discussed in detail in a later chapter.)

Temperament type merely identifies our most natural or favorite way of responding to people and situations. Even though we may feel strange or awkward as we consult the third and fourth functions—our shadow side arenas—we benefit from the practice and use of the always available preference-helpers. Engaging the lesser preferences gets easier with purposeful use.

For your convenience, I've included the innate patterns (cycles) for each Personality Type on page 53. You'll find it is really fun when you realize which preference you are actually using with particular people and situations.

Purposely using less preferred preferences encourages healthy balance and enables better handling of different situations, producing a clearer and more beautiful melody. We can obtain "visas" any time to enter the arenas of our less preferred functions. For instance, if you are a strong iNtuitive, you'll be wise to purposely include some hands-on Sensing chores such as cleaning the garage or weeding the garden.

Sensing folks are usually not as interested in the following overview, but I'm including it to satisfy any curiosity and deeper understanding about the order with which we use each preference. (iNtuitives like to delve deeper into the unknown.) The eventual benefit of understanding the individuality of each preference and when to access it contributes mightily to getting along with everyone.

And, applying the list below to your particular preferences will simply give you relief in explaining why you enjoy writing more than raking leaves, or why you prefer following a recipe or making up a new one, or why you work before you play, etc.

1. Everyone extroverts (uses on others) their last letter—**J** or **P**.
2. **J** reflects decision making—Thinking (Head-Logic) or Feeling (Heart-Logic).
3. **P** reflects information gathering—Sensing (Hands-on) or iNtuition (Mind-on-Ideas).
4. Extroverts' last letter is their favorite preference to use on others—which can result in failing to develop their second preference.
5. Introverts' last letter is their second favorite preference—and becomes their best developed function, for example:

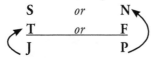

6. Introverts prefer to reserve their first and favorite preference for private use.
7. Since introverts are forced to use their second preference through Extroversion, they develop both the first and second functions.
8. Opposite our first preference is our fourth (least) preference.
9. Opposite our second preference is our third, or tertiary, preference.

ISFJ	ESFJ	INFJ	ENFJ
I	E	I	E
S1 N4	S2 N3	N1 S4	N2 S3
F2 T3	F1 T4	F2 T3	F1 T4
J P	J P	J P	J P
ISFP	**ESFP**	**INFP**	**ENFP**
I	E	I	E
S2 N3	S1 N4	N2 S3	N1 S4
F1 T4	F2 T3	F1 T4	F2 T3
P J	P J	P J	P J
ESTP	**ESTJ**	**INTJ**	**ENTJ**
E	E	I	E
S1 N4	S2 N3	N1 S4	N2 S3
T2 F3	T1 F4	T2 F3	T1 F4
P J	J P	J P	J P
ISTJ	**ESTP**	**INTP**	**ENTP**
I	E	I	E
S1 N4	S1 N4	N2 S3	N1 S4
T2 F3	T2 F3	T1 F4	T2 F3
J P	P J	P J	P J

CHAPTER 3

God's Garden: Seedbed for Communication

Each one should test his own actions.
Then he can take pride in himself,
without comparing himself to somebody else,
for each one should carry his own load.
Galatians 6:4-5

Sometimes we are so aware of what we are not that we fail to appreciate who we are. Parents often approve of their offspring only when they are replicas of themselves—a very unfair and shortsighted view. Do you really want two of you? As hard as some of us might try, we just can't become a carbon copy. This futile attempt can turn a home into the primary source for low self-esteem.

Healthy self-image begins with understanding and appreciating our personality and its instinctive preferences. But until we mature enough to understand that each person is unique in every way and possibly quite different from parents, siblings, partners, and even friends, years of feeling inferior and weird are likely to mar our self-worth. In my experience using the MBTI, no one has ever disliked their personality type. If anything, they wished more people were just like them.

More Unique Than Flowers

Did you ever wonder why, as creative as God is, many people assume he merely created two kinds of people—male and female? How boring and how untrue!

For hundreds of years sociologists, writers, and religious leaders have stereotyped men as rough, rugged, and right and women as weak, weepy, and wrong. As stated earlier and baring repeating, only recently has our culture dared to accept behavior reflecting 40 percent of men as innately tenderhearted (Feelers) and 40 percent of women as tough-minded (Thinkers). Both males and females can share like preferences with joy if understood.

Because this phenomenon is generally not accepted nor appreciated, I've been inspired to address it so these very special people can be legitimately celebrated. The entire population is blessed by Heart-Logic men and Head-Logic women.

Consider the varieties of flowers that God has meticulously fashioned. The daffodil alone has more than 40 varieties. Talk about individuality! Do you really think when it comes to humans that God would have limited his creativity to just two types? Imagine flowers as having personalities that fill a garden with endless varieties and special gifts. Might we not hear that:

• geraniums desire to be delicate like portulaca?
• marigolds yearn to smell as sweet as gardenias?
• violets aspire to be hardy, like zinnias?
• petunias crave as bounteous production as chrysanthemums?
• sunflowers act proud for their height and popularity of seeds?
• poppies brag about their radiant colors and unique contribution to the world?

Personalities differ even more than flowers, and the differences are extremely more complex. Subtle variations within each personality type preferences—arenas, as I also refer to them—are also very distinguishable. No two people are exactly alike, even though they may share the same preferences in the four major areas discussed in the previous chapters.

As I have done in other books, I will use a well-known activity as an aid in making clear application of the truths we will discover. Since flowers, like music, speak a universal language, we will pretend that we are part of a huge flower garden—God's. Each personality has a flower name that has a degree of resemblance for just an extra little handle for emphasis.

We will envision what growing in a flower garden with 16 different varieties might be like. Each type needs sunshine, water, and nourishment, though in different amounts. Flowers battle bugs, weeds, and normal garden woes. Some flowers may pair off, only to discover that their needs are different and that they require extra attention for blending. The beauty of a flower garden is in the eye of the beholder. But the real beauty of this exercise is the promised joyous amazement and surprise as you understand your uniqueness and that of others and also gain the skill of getting along with everyone.

We should have lots of fun observing these colorful—some strong, private, sensitive but complex—flowers. Enjoy your flower-mate, realizing that no variety is either inferior or superior. The labels describing the main characteristic of each four-letter type are borrowed from my brief profiles in *Self-Esteem: Gift from God.*

ISFJ	Tulip	steady, organized, gorgeous, brightly colored	Servers
ISFP	Rose	independent, private, popular, vibrant colors	Sympathizers
ISTJ	Aster	tall, strong, bright red, white, orange, pink, purple	Conscientious Workers
ISTP	Gladiolus	strong, stately, run the gamut of rainbow colors	Unstoppable
ESFJ	Zinnia	strong, hardy, various heights, bold colors	Hosts and Hostesses
ESFP	Daisy	hardy, cheerful, popular, pastel colors	Performers
ESTJ	Geranium	sturdy, dependable, a host of colors	Organizers
ESTP	Hollyhock	tall, hardy, adaptable, vibrant, multicolors	Physical Rescuers
INFJ	Camelia	delicate, private, red, white, multicolors	Empathizers
INFP	Portulaca	complex, jubilant borders, many distinct colors	Idealists
INTJ	Iris	stately, sturdy, private, multi-colors, even black	Expert Strategists
INTP	Delphinium	tall, independent, private, blues, pinks, purples	Think-tank Experts
ENFJ	Poppy	versatile, single or double blossoms, array of colors	Encouragers
ENFP	Chrysanthemum	hardy, versatile, many colors	Catalysts
ENTJ	Sunflower	strong, hardy, bright, yellow, variety of colors	Head Chiefs
ENTP	Hibiscus	tall, awesome, brilliant colors	Powerful People Movers

Combating Low Self-Esteem by Sharpening Communication

Low self-esteem seems to be a worldwide malady of major proportions, surpassing alcoholism, drug abuse, lack of education, or financial problems. Experiences in family counseling convinced me years ago that low self-esteem is at the root of many marriage failures, family grievances, church squabbles, and even poor mental and physical health.

Actually, the critical problem with which we all grapple is lack of open, kind, and productive communication. If anyone has ever given you the silent treatment, walked out, screamed, or called you names, you know what I mean.

Inadequate or negative communication breeds isolation, misunderstandings, and feelings of rejection. It contributes little to friendships or problem solving. In fact, open communication is what strings people together and makes living worth-while. Good communication is not only casual conversation, but also honest sharing and listening.

Some risk may be involved in this. Satisfactory communication takes time, effort, mutual respect, courage, and healthy self-esteem. Edifying communication is a skill to be sharpened. Check out the following complaints related to the absence of good communication that I hear most often from unhappy counselees:

- "He reads the paper or watches TV; he's not interested in what I have to say."
- "The cell phone monopolizes her attention."
- "The only time we ever talk is when we fight over money, sex, or relatives."
- "My teenage daughter disappears into her room or leaves with friends."
- "I don't understand my boss."
- "No one understands me."
- "My parents just criticize how we parent our children."
- "I just can't talk to my parents."
- "My sister and I are on different wave lengths."
- "Someone's feelings are always getting hurt at work."
- "His face is always buried in his cell phone, iPad, or tablet."

A significant part of the tenderhearted, Feeling, decision makers' self-esteem hinges on receiving positive feedback about what they are, do, and say from bosses, spouses, parents, co-workers, or friends. These people tend to measure their worth by the amount of dialogue with others.

Low self-esteem and lack of communication are interrelated. Many break-ups are directly related to disenchantment between partners. Communication is often traced to our preoccupation with such fast-paced, single pursuits as running, aerobics, and workouts, and to the disappearance of mealtimes—the natural setting for conversation—to say nothing about the electronic addiction of our world.

"Can you help me find a home for Twila?" a new counselee pleaded. "We can't stand her."

"Before we proceed with that request," I responded, "I'd like to give you and your husband the MBTI to help our communication." I also requested a session with Twila, which revealed to me that she was not only a delightful child but also very different from the rest of her family. I did find five families who were willing to take her in. Here's what happened:

Ten-year-old Twila was upsetting her family with her chronic stomach pains, headaches, temper tantrums, and resistance to attending school. They regarded Twila's tears and immature behavior as manipulative, a little weird, inferior, and certainly unacceptable. They believed it was up to Twila to grow up and fall in line. "Why can't you be more like your sister?" her parents asked. Even her grandmother asked her not to visit. Her father questioned whether she belonged to him.

When I chatted with Twila alone I learned that she resisted school because of the kids pushing at the bus stop, noise on the bus, and yelling of her gym teacher. And because she finished assignments first, the teacher directed students who were not finished to receive help from her, which she resented. She preferred to read a book with earned leftover time.

At home her sister would say, "Don't step into my room and mess it up," and would criticize her outfits, but never offered to assist her in choosing something different. My giving Twila a daily journal assignment for the next appointment excited her.

When her exasperated parents returned for another session, I suggested that before they find an adoptive home they allow me to give them the Myers-Briggs Type Indicator. After they heard the interpretation and saw the results, the lights came on.

The mom, dad, and older sister typed out the same: Introverted-Sensing-Thinking-Structured (ISTJ). This meant Twila's mom and sister were Thinkers, a minority preference for females. Twila's family overpowered her. News and sports monopolized the family television but never programs that appealed to Twila. Since the rest of the family enjoyed hands-on chores, they assumed Twila should. They received approval from themselves as they finished jobs and projects. They had little sympathy for a slacker or whiner, as they called Twila.

Twila's Introverted-iNtuitive-Feeling-sPpontaneous (INFP) type was opposite of her family's in three areas. Twila needed tender attention, approval, affection, encouragement, and harmony. She preferred warm animal programs such as *Lassie* and reading and playing. That's why she couldn't be like her sister who kept a neat room and always put things away. In a class of 42 students, Twila's type wasn't even represented.

With this new language of communication and appreciation, it wasn't long before the family got the picture of what Twila had been going through. Twila's hostility was a legitimate cry for praise, dialogue, and tender loving care—all unnatural needs for their own type.

Twila's family members began to administer emotional first-aid by taking interest in her abilities and acknowledging her feelings and fears. They encouraged her love for reading by taking her to the library. Her parents gave her creative chores such as feeding and walking the dog, baking, and redecorating her room.

The angry outbursts and tears quickly subsided as her parents, sister, and teachers began to understand the legitimate differences as pointed out by the MBTI information. Twila was set free to be the person she was created to be. Today, Twila is a college-educated professional health care worker and a writer. What might have become of Twila?

Communication Styles

Until a person understands and appreciates how and why others think, feel, and act, conversation will most likely be inappropriate or misinterpreted. And unless the person who desires to improve relationships is secure enough to risk being misunderstood or rejected, successful communication may remain a dream.

Head-Logic Thinking vs. Heart-Logic Feeling

Head-Logic Thinkers prefer brief logical exchanges that are primarily situation-based rather than people- or feeling-based. They dislike wading through volumes of nonessential information that could be trimmed in the interest of relevancy.

Heart-Logic Feelers who often "beat around the bush" annoy Thinkers, who are apt to regard good communication as the absence of discussion and argument. Thinkers trust their decisions and expect others to do the same. They cannot agree to anything for which they do not see good reason. "Don't ask questions: just do what I say" is the motto of most Thinkers, but it is hardly conducive to comfortable conversation. Even logical decisions can often be improved.

Although attracted to Thinkers, Feeling decision makers often lack the courage and self-esteem to challenge cold logic. "I'm afraid to disagree," many Feelers have shared. Ironically, that people are afraid of them never ceases to amaze Thinkers, who actually regard themselves as fairly soft when necessary. Thinkers say they do not like to argue, but they just can't stand to be wrong. Don't be afraid of them! They all have a soft spot inside. They need, want, and expect our trust and respect.

Feelers, who are not eager to buck decisive Thinkers but want harmonious communication, first need to have their points and facts well in mind or on paper, then gather their courage and practice brevity as they converse with their opposites. I have discovered that it takes at least two Feeling individuals to sway a Thinker's logic.

On the other hand, Thinkers do well to meet Feelers halfway by learning to tolerate a dose of nonessentials and endeavoring to soften their bluntness.

"If I would just hear him say 'I love you' once in a while. I would feel so much better," a Feeler said. However, the thinking partner would probably respond, "I don't have to repeat something that hasn't changed."

Normally, Thinkers are rather confident and need only occasional verbal approval of who they are or what they have already decided or accomplished. If they are to open the communication channels, they need to learn to verbally affirm their counterparts on a regular basis.

"The house is a mess, and I'm not used to that," Bill griped to his wife. "What did you do all day, for heaven's sake?" Bill sees no tangible sign of housekeeping excellence and smells no food cooking, all familiar memories from his childhood.

Jan feels intimidated by his loaded question, so she becomes obstinate and private about her activities. "I'm not against housework," Jan defended. "I've been involved most of the day driving Mrs. Dillon to and from a doctor's appointment. I feel that helping her is more important than doing something for ourselves," she added sarcastically.

Bill needs to applaud Jan, a Feeling person who would put in 36 straight hours of caring for someone in need without a complaint. But she also needs his approval. Thinkers could quell much intimidation and also improve their image and popularity by affirming "I love you" and saying "I'm sorry" or "I think you are a super person" when appropriate. Any person who desires the dividend of trust and respect must invest in the virtues of consideration and tenderness.

Put Thinking and Introversion together and you have the quietest people in the world! Introverted Thinkers are not actually anti-dialogue, but find talking quite draining and even painful. Often such people come across as stern, unfriendly, and no-nonsense. Even though sharing personal feelings is unnatural for them, they will respond readily when they discover someone with whom they can entrust their confidences.

Introverted Thinkers need to understand how their silence intimidates the Feeling segment, including those who are confident extroverts, and should also consider how important it is to their friends, co-workers, and especially their partners and children to hear their voices and share ideas, feelings, and foolishness and do a little laughing.

Extroverted Thinkers can more easily tolerate people and conversation, but they, too, prefer brief, logical discussions. Since they rely on ear editing, they often make verbal errors.

Thinkers need to endeavor to listen to more chatter than they would normally choose and to share miscellaneous tidbits of information so as to comply somewhat with Feeling people's expectations and their gauge of personal worth.

The other 50 percent of the general population, Heart-Logic Feeling decision makers of both genders, require small talk but also hunger for limited in-depth communication. Feelers are quite capable of appropriating logic when necessary.

The softhearted segment can rightly be called information bearers. As soon as they receive interesting data, they have a compulsion to pass it along. Because warmhearted people find it easy to share news, even when the subject has not come up naturally, many need to develop discipline in discretionary sharing.

Tenderhearted types are constantly wondering if they are meeting with the approval of important others; they would like affirmation. They measure their worth by the amount of dialogue from their counterparts. Feelers thrive on verbal or written praise for who they are and for products made and services rendered. They say to others what they expect to hear or have done in return.

Since few Thinkers understand the complexity of Feelers' expectations, spoken and unspoken, the latter suffer tremendously and needlessly from hurt feelings, anger, resentments, and low self-esteem. On the other hand, harmony lovers need to keep in mind that insisting on peace at any price may also be shortcutting someone else's growth in maturity and responsibility.

When the tenderhearted are also introverts, they prefer limited conversation and fewer people. Communication is not easy for them, yet they need it so much! Usually they prefer talking with one person at a time and often prefer to put their feelings and opinions on paper. They are usually very patient listeners who attract extroverts who want to talk.

Quiet and sensitive people are unlikely to reveal their emotional needs without some encouragement. Thus, without others' knowledge, their self-esteem often drastically sags—which might explain why the majority of counseling is done with this group.

Extroverted Sensing-Feelers are the talkers of this world. In fact, some have a tendency to drown everyone in words. Unfortunately, some of these people have difficulty listening because they are so busy planning what they want to say next. The mere ability to talk, however, does not mean that one appreciates or utilizes communication skills.

A good habit in serious dialogue is to repeat what the speaker just said: "I hear you saying…" This not only teaches us to listen carefully but also guarantees that listeners have sifted accurately through extensive verbiage.

Because Feelers are sensitive to criticism and are easily put on the defensive, many are often verbally at each other's throats when decisions are involved. Skilled dialogue modifies many such clashes. Since the softhearted segment desires peaceful communication and is willing to patiently soothe, encourage, and counsel through written and spoken word, Thinkers should be willing to do their part in appreciating the softhearted and emulating their sensitivity.

iNtuitive vs. Sensing

Our favorite way of gathering information also influences the subject matter of conversation we most appreciate. The Sensing hands-on crowd prefers chronological data, a linear description of facts and events as they actually occurred. Their factual account of stories and events will nearly always be accurate and make sense, and they can repeat these stories exactly. Their iNtuitive friends prefer to discuss ideas helically, in a spiral or circular fashion that hits the high points first and saves supporting facts until last.

Repeating something verbatim is not only difficult for iNtuitives, but also very boring. The facts, names, and fall of events may alter when repeated, not because these people are deceitful, but because iNtuitives prefer to emphasize principles or present the big picture rather than focus on factual details.

Though iNtuitives are often suspected of tampering with the truth, they usually do so unintentionally, because they honestly don't remember how much or when. Of course, anyone, no matter what type, is capable of deliberately misstating facts or stretching the truth.

When we know what type of person we are addressing, transferring information according to the method the other prefers will aid communication. Hopefully, the other person will do the same for us.

An iNtuitive and a Sensing person may experience poor communication because they function in different arenas. Even if they are both also extroverts, they need help in learning how to relate to and receive information from their partner. For example, I attempt to get all my facts straight before I discuss a new idea or purchase with my husband, who prefers Sensing facts and figures. I usually list the items on paper. It's easier for me speak in his style than to expect him to adjust to my circular way of conversation.

Probably the best communicators are extroverts who also prefer to operate on iNtuitive and Feeling levels (ENF). However, although they regard people as being of highest importance and priority, they may take communication for granted, believing they are understood and their explanations and ideas are accepted. Extroverted iNtuitives are usually able to discuss their own and others' problems at length and fairly easily.

Structured vs. sPontaneous

Conversation, and thus communication, is also affected by a person's lifestyle preference. Structured people like to know things ahead of time so that they have time to think over facts and details and get ready, whereas sPontaneous people become burdened with too much beforehand information and have a tendency to forget

details. This is probably because they are always sitting on go and want nothing to threaten their freedom of action.

My research shows that sPontaneous people seem to enjoy the process of conversation; Structured people just want to get it finished and move on to the next item on their agenda. Many Structured counselees complain that the sPontaneous people in their lives choose to discuss a problem immediately rather than scheduling a talk for later, when there would be sufficient or quality time.

Watering the Seedbed

The miraculous improvement in communication after people understand the designed differences in personality leaves no doubt that we are on the right track in building self-esteem. Until we respect ourselves, we will not respect anyone else. True, the response we get from others does affect our self-esteem, but if the foundation of our self-image is based on recognizing our unique gifting, we are better prepared to adjust to others' lack of appreciation for us as individuals.

Healthy self-esteem is necessary for everyone. When Jesus said, "Love others as you love yourself," he assumed that our acceptance and appreciation of ourselves would be projected toward others in positive actions and words—through the water of communication in our people-garden.

Next to air, water is the most important necessity for existence. Yet it is so often taken for granted that we seldom realize how essential or precious it is until the well runs dry. Bitter battles have been fought for the possession of some muddy waterhole or tiny stream. So, too, emotionally thirsty people search for life-refreshing communication to quench their dry, neglected, and crushed spirits.

To have a beautiful garden, one doesn't just aimlessly sow seeds or dump bulbs on the ground and then sit back and watch something gorgeous happen. A healthy array of flowers is the result of soil preparation, pruning, fertilizing, spraying, weeding, tilling and, certainly, skillful watering. The same principles apply as we blend the temperamentally unique specimens in God's garden of humanity.

Applying understanding and appreciation is like mixing light and air with water to assure a garden's growth. The goal of this study is to increase the understanding and appreciation that encourage effective communication, with the overall aim of improving the quality of relationships at all levels. These ideas have been tested and tried by hundreds of people. And they work! We can learn to appreciate and get along with everyone.

CHAPTER 4

Expectations:
Bugs in Our Garden

A man's spirit sustains him in sickness, but a crushed spirit who can bear?
The heart of the discerning acquires knowledge; the ears of the wise seek it out.
Proverbs 18:14-15

This study is written for those who want to strive to do their best and realize their potential, but also for those who wish to encourage others to make the most of the priceless gift of life: their abilities and personality.

The information I have gathered from every type of person, from various economic and educational backgrounds and assorted age groups, indicates that expectations are somewhat like bugs in a garden. There are lots of them—everywhere, and in various shapes and colors. Some bugs are beneficial and some destructive; some are big and some so small they can barely be seen.

Like bugs, expectations—whether subtle, unspoken, imagined, or expressed— wield almost unbelievable influence on communication and life itself. Identifying the various categories is a necessary first step toward building and maintaining healthy self-esteem in our communities.

If we did a word-association test on expectations, the responses would range from positive to strongly negative. Certain expectations are healthy and good. For example, encouraging children to love to learn and to respect hard work is the privileged duty of parents and teachers. Urging young people to aim high and realize their potential so as to be independent and successful is a built-in assignment that has its own rewards for adults. All this involves developing the right kind of expectations. We all need a lot of help in getting along with everyone.

Granted, some people set no goals or put any expectation on themselves or their children. Perhaps it is because no one held out reachable expectations for them. Others seem to require no outside encouragement to strive for excellence. There are those who are faithfully and positively challenged but still choose mere survival. When a person's self-esteem is low or unhealthy, he or she usually does not plan for the future or set challenging personal goals.

Some expectations may come across as threatening and vindictive and thereby produce guilt, inadequacy, anger, and resentment—most of which can kill the spirit of anyone in their grip. Expecting children to be number one may frighten them into underachievement. A fine line of balance must be drawn between aspirations and reality—which includes one's abilities and temperament.

David's dad, a doctor, insisted his son always wear a coat and tie to public school because some day he would be a doctor or perhaps a lawyer, like his uncle. Although dressing up was not in style at David's school, he obeyed Dad's rules. However, David eventually chose not to go to college and now runs a successful little business where he wears tennis shoes and a t-shirt.

Understanding variety in temperament provides clues toward the kind of expectations and challenges others are likely to appreciate and respond to. For instance, most iNtuitives would find it very frustrating to be expected to excel in a Sensing, hands-on occupation.

Pete described his experiences: "I tried my dad's business, but failed. He's the VP of a national lending institution and wanted me to step into a financially secure career like my brother did, but I just couldn't get into figures and offices. I wanted to please him and didn't want to seem ungrateful, but it just didn't work. We got on each other's nerves. I just wasn't happy. I do enjoy designing home interiors, though. I don't make as much, but I look forward to going to work. Dad still doesn't understand. He says, 'Someday you'll come around.'"

Children who reject involvement in a family business or a parent's profession often create a bitter pill for their elders to swallow, but many family feuds are avoided when parents recognize that their offspring may have different expectations from their own.

Many Sensing people directed and shoved toward iNtuitive careers such as counseling or the ministry experience the same level of frustration, as did Rick who explained, "All my brothers are ministers. My parents have told me a million times that at birth they dedicated me for full-time religious work. But I am not that comfortable around people and really enjoy being a CPA. Even though I am the treasurer for our church, that doesn't satisfy them."

Some parents are extremely disappointed and fearful when their children resist going to college or fail while there. Of course, college isn't for everyone, but a college education in most cases is a wise investment of time and money. The discipline of study and exposure to new ideas and learning prepares students for an unknown future. (For in-depth help in parenting using Myers-Briggs information, you may want to consult mine and my husband's book *Coaching Kids: Practical Tips for Effective Communication*).

Just as some people are better off in non-college pursuits, others are more fulfilled by remaining single and/or childless. Heavy family expectations in these areas produce disappointment, disagreement, and eventually deep-seated resentment on both sides.

Self-Imposed Expectations

Nearly everyone says at one time or another, "I should do or be this or that." Self-imposed expectations are helpful when they involve such goals as planning a career, pursuing an education, learning a job, getting up for work, studying for a test, finishing a project, or taking care of children or possessions. Unfortunately, many people spend their lives correcting mistakes or enslaved to appetites that require tremendous financial support. Sometimes a person is kept from doing what he or she really enjoys doing until late in life.

If you have chosen to be a parent, student, employee, or provider and later discover you don't want to do the things you have obligated yourself to do, you must work on changing your "wanter."

Motivating ourselves to accomplish what falls within our responsibility is synonymous with maturity. The energizing stress that comes from doing what appeals to us or is in line with reachable goals is a positive innovator.

Basically, human beings are lazy, as Scott Peck addresses in *The Road Less Traveled*. He goes so far as to identify original sin as laziness. The opposite of laziness is not perfection, but love. His perspective is refreshing and right on target.

It surprises many of us to discover that even highly Structured people sometimes have to scold and cajole themselves into doing what they know is theirs to do. We all struggle with having to change our "wanters." Being consistently disciplined is a tough assignment for everyone. Sensing people have a tendency to delay dealing with long-range possibilities while iNtuitives may have to muster up motivation when the obligation involves physical routine.

The sPontaneous crowd, usually very responsive to unexpected and exciting challenges, is obliged to struggle more than anyone in this area. You see, we're all basically in the same pickle, regardless of our temperament.

The kind of self-imposed expectations we want to analyze here are those that are unrealistic, or in opposition to our particular type of temperament. Self-imposed expectations produce harmful stress, which destroys self-confidence and inhibits communication—the bad kind of bugs in our garden.

Many of us are guilty of deciding what we want to be or do without regard for our particular situation or temperament. We are then disappointed if we don't or can't measure up to our mental goal or standard in ways such as these:

- "I should keep the house as perfect as when I didn't have an outside job."
- "I must maintain straight A's at college online, even though I work full time."
- "I've got to make a certain number of sales this week."
- "I must not be like my irresponsible father in any way."

- "Since my sister blew it, I'm determined to make my folks proud of me."
- "I need to maintain the standard of living my parents had."
- "My children deserve my unlimited time."
- "Everyone must like me."
- "I should hand-make all the gifts I give like my sister does."
- "I'm going to reach the top financially."
- "My opinions and ideas must be highly respected by all my friends."

Many women employed outside the home put unrealistic expectations on themselves to be super moms and wives. It is humanly improbable, even in a two-parent family, to work 40 hours a week away from home, prepare balanced meals, assist children with homework, fulfill chauffeuring duties, and still have some private time for self, spouse, and friends.

Our nation teems with single parents who are inclined to over-compensate for the absence of the other parent and thus subject themselves to guilt-producing unreasonable expectations. These people, predominantly women, eventually suffer low self-esteem and experience burnout.

Many men unconsciously struggle to disprove what dad always said, "You'll never amount to anything," by working 50-60 hours a week. Others are pressured by the educational, prestigious, or financial achievements of their siblings or parents. It is a given that most children vie for parental blessing, often unsuccessfully. Surprisingly, many adults struggle all their lives to gain the approval of their parents. All they really want to hear is "I'm proud of you and love you." Some of these unexamined expectations must be settled posthumously through counseling.

Some tend to lay on themselves the goal of never failing. Others often contend relentlessly for success, trust, and respect by their peers and superiors. Many Feeling persons aim to satisfy and please everyone, striving for faultless living so they will be liked by everyone.

"Do you tolerate anyone, Sandy?" I asked a counselee. "Yes," she said sheepishly. "Do you suppose, then, that anyone has to tolerate you?" "Oh, I hope not," Sandy shivered. "I want everyone to like me."

"We don't like ourselves all the time. How can we expect others to like us all the time?" I queried. "I don't know," Sandy hesitated. "I just assumed that good people are liked by all."

If we expect ourselves never to say a disagreeable word or dislike anyone, we'll never like or approve of ourselves totally. We can get along with anyone but may not be comfortable spending extended time with certain individuals.

"When we don't measure up to our own expectations," an iNtuitive group member shared, "we are likely to get discouraged with who we are and want to throw in the towel."

iNtuitives have to be especially careful to separate expectations from idealistic aspirations. We all need goals of some kind, but setting unreal expectations for ourselves is most often counterproductive.

Structured people—whether Sensing or iNtuitive—have been known to make lists a mile long for Saturday, their only day off. When they don't complete their list for whatever reason—good or bad—they condemn themselves. They seldom leave time for play and become angry with themselves for not completing their scheduled tasks.

On the other hand, sPontaneous people seem better able to resist the daily pressure of self-imposed expectations because of their characteristic resistance to schedules and plans. But they will still suffer overall self-condemnation if their responsibilities or achievements fall below what they expected of themselves.

Analyze your self-imposed expectations to make sure you are being realistic. Many of the things we expect ourselves to do, say, or become are unreasonable—unless we are in training for "Super Person" of the year. Self-drawn expectations are rarely challenged by others, so we need to learn to ask ourselves:

- "Is this something I really want?"
- "What is my motivation for wanting this?"
- "Why do I expect myself to achieve these goals?"
- "Is this a reasonable expectation for myself?"
- "Does the outcome warrant the energy expended?"
- "Does the expectation violate my temperament preferences?"
- "Is my personal expectation hurting others?"
- "Am I physically and mentally able to fulfill this expectation?"
- "Does it really add depth and meaning to my life?"

Imagined Expectations

Many of our expectations are superfluous since they reflect only our imagined concept of aspirations others have previously set. Feeling types seem to have more problems handling imagined expectations because of their eagerness to please others and receive approval.

Some of our imagined expectations parallel the list of the self-imposed ones already described. We may assume someone else expects us to do something, when this is not so. For example, I have always taken personal pride in unlocking the front door when I hear Jim drive up, knowing that he usually has his hands full. I assumed he expected me to unlock the door and greet him.

I decided to test my own suggestions about the validity of assumed expectations. When I asked him if he indeed expected me to unlock the door, to my surprise he said, "No, I don't. In fact, it bothers me when you do because I already have my keys out."

My guilt was lessened, but my feelings were a little hurt at his answer. "But I thought you expected me to greet you whenever you came home," I challenged.

"That's your idea," he said. "Actually, I feel a bit crowded when you meet me. I'm usually deep in thought and prefer a little space."

Jim knows that I like to be greeted and assisted with packages at the door. I had just assumed that he did, too. But Thinkers are not as sensitive as Feelers about being greeted and assisted!

Harry, a tenderhearted male teacher, identified an imagined expectation: "My coworkers have asked me every year, 'What job have you found for the summer?' I realize, after all these years, that rather than taking the summers to read, relax, study, and prepare curriculum for the next year, I've given in to peer pressure and found a job because I supposed, since my coworkers expected it, that it was the right thing to do."

Harry's teacher friends have no idea what pressure they unconsciously exerted on their coworker. "It's my problem," Harry admitted. "I chose to be controlled by what I imagined were others' expectations. Yet, I resented and blamed them for those unfulfilling summers. It feels good now to be in charge of making my own vacation decisions."

The truth is, trying to live up to expectations that we imagine others have put on us is unhealthy pressure that later could take a toll. Distinguishing between imagined and real expectations requires simply checking with the person or group. Communication will clear the air and destroy tension. Asking ourselves those "what" and "why" questions can purify our motives and release us from any self-made boxes of guilt.

Unspoken Expectations

Many people create serious relationship problems by silently expecting or hoping for certain behaviors or favors from others and then keeping those expectations a mystery, as the following example shows.

The Nelsons are in business together. Lois' expectations of Larry have been unreasonable in many respects. She likes to be with him and appreciates his business skills, but she's not easy to please. Lois expects Larry to say just the right thing (by her standards). She prefers that he stay in the inner office to keep him away from customers to whom he might make a statement she would disapprove. Introverted

Lois needs to keep in mind that because Larry is extroverted, he will likely say many things she regards as unnecessary.

This female partner expects her male co-worker to do the proper thing by helping her only when she wants help. This would require that Larry read her mind since she doesn't express herself easily. Lois needs to verbalize to Larry what she expects of him. Then he can tell her whether or not he agrees and is willing to comply.

Lois also thinks that Larry only pretends not to know what is going on around him. She complains that he doesn't pick up what she regards as strong hints about things that need doing, but she needs to remember that because Larry is an iNtuitive, he will not be as observant as she is about the physical world. Larry gets lost in the idea world from time to time, which is quite normal for an iNtuitive. But they've never discussed these issues.

Here's another example of how unspoken expectations upset relationships:

"I expect John to come right home after work," Lila said. "I call him at 3:00 to make sure he's coming home on time and he'll say 'yes'—then won't show up until 8:00."

Understanding that John, an introverted sPontaneous iNtuitive, gets bored at work when events bubble along too smoothly, he unconsciously creates crises to satisfy his boredom. Then he has to spend time unraveling what he began. His hunger for excitement violates Lila's Feeling, Sensing, and Structure preferences.

Changing her plans so as to satisfy John's preference for no schedule intimidates Lila, which then keeps her from voicing her expectations. John has no idea she is under so much stress. His inconsideration is mostly because Lila has allowed herself to be intimidated, rather than honestly making plain what she expects. Her problem was solved by learning how they were different and meeting each other halfway. They have learned to discuss expectations.

Expectations that we put on others without informing them—or expectations that others privately put on us—cause tremendous problems in communication. When we assume that certain things will be said or done and those expectations go unfulfilled, many of us, especially Feeling people, are likely to get upset, hurt, and suffer rejection or resentment.

Thinkers are more likely to be bothered rather than disappointed. A question such as "Where were you last night? We came to see you" lays guilt on the people who were away. These visitors actually expected their friends to be home and are unjustifiably resentful because their unspoken expectations were unmet.

Elaine came from a home where no arguments were allowed, yet disagreements in her husband's home were as normal as hugs and kisses. This couple will need to discuss their differences openly and arrive at a creative compromise.

Some tenderhearted people seem to expect others to mistreat them. They even help them out by constantly condemning and faulting themselves. These people need to communicate their expectations so others can either reject the expectations or embrace the now-spoken desires. Criticism follows when expectations are unmet, or any time someone is put on the defensive. The following examples of assumed expectations also take the smile out of relationships:

- New club officers will function like their predecessors.
- Employees will always turn reports in on time.
- Children will keep their rooms straight.
- Guests will check your schedule before they drop in.
- Gift recipients will write acknowledgment notes.
- Grandparents will provide unlimited and last-minute babysitting.
- Anniversaries and birthdays will be remembered.

Once someone renders a service, benefactors are likely to assume that it is part of the regular program, as in these familiar situations:

- making the coffee at work
- calling in or picking up the lunch order
- running forgotten items to school
- doing the laundry
- waking family members for work or school
- picking up clutter
- preparing meals
- answering the phone
- locking or unlocking the doors
- fueling and maintaining vehicles
- keeping up the yard
- running errands
- chauffeuring non-drivers

When a client concerned about distancing from his partner sent a copy of his expectations for his partner, I was blown away not only by the long list but also by how demeaning, unfair, and controlling they were. No wonder she left.

Compile your own list of expectations that you assume others put on you, and then one for unspoken expectations that you put on other people. This could be an excellent family or work exercise to stimulate communication and dispel tensions.

Thinkers generally figure that people do something because they like to do it or accept it as their duty. If no one complains, Thinkers assume that everything is okay and that the "workers" are happy. By way of contrast, Feeling people primarily say and do for others what they themselves want to hear and have done. When others don't reciprocate or even appreciate their services, they feel mistreated and unappreciated.

The Bible instructs us to "do to others what you would have them do to you" (the Golden Rule, Matt. 7:12). Many Feeling types might respond, "I do and do for others, and no one does for me." No one likes being taken for granted.

"Every time you need a pat on the back, give it to yourself and consider it from me," one Thinker said to his Feeling counterpart. "I'll tell you when I'm displeased with you," he promised. That sort of attitude is not enough for Feeling people, especially those who believe that they go beyond the call of duty in the many little things they feel obligated to do, even though they enjoy being needed. Acknowledgement works wonders.

Many Feeling individuals hold their breath before a special day, hoping against hope that loved ones will remember the day. Feeling hearts ache when they receive no recognition. This holds true for Feeling men and boys who expect the same kind of attention, praise, appreciation, and thanks that tenderhearted females do. It is hard enough to fulfill expressed expectations, but to hope that others will read our minds is unrealistic and even unfair. (Send cards and reminders of your birthday if you do not want to be totally disappointed.)

Expressed Expectations

Expectations that are expressed in one way or another are the easiest kind to identify and deal with. They come in assorted styles and can both communicate desires and engender a variety of reactions, such as these blunt statements:

- "Too bad you're not like your sister."
- "Can't you hear the baby crying?"
- "I'll wait for your call as soon as you get home."
- "These reports must go out tonight."
- "The least you could do is clean up your mess."
- "I'll need a ride home."

Some expressed expectations include words such as should, ought, must, and need—which I identify as war words—and "I thought" statements:

- "You should have waited for me."
- "I thought you'd get me up."
- "You need to figure out who's going to pay for it."
- "You ought to get started on your studies."
- "You must find a better doctor."
- "You should feed your kids more vegetables."

Then, there are the guilt-inducing questions that spew out so thoughtlessly and mechanically from all temperaments, genders, and ages. We've all heard and used them ourselves:

- "You don't mind handling those details, do you?"
- "You're coming for Thanksgiving this year, aren't you?"
- "Mom, you washed my jeans, didn't you?"
- "Don't you ever look at the gas gauge?"
- "You don't mind checking my mailbox, do you?"
- "We can count on you to be there, can't we?"
- "Do you have time to water my plants?"

When considering expressed expectations, don't forget a couple of reminders. First, be careful with your speech, both what you say to others and to yourself: keep it totally honest.

In the introduction of my *Self-Esteem* book I tell about a man who came for help in dealing with a difficult marriage. In the course of getting acquainted I said, "Tell me about your father." The man began to weep and told this story:

"When I was 10, I botched a chore my father gave me to do and he said to me, 'I'm so ashamed of you that I'm not going to tell my friends that you're my son.' Those words are always in my mind, every day," he said with a choked voice.

Just 17 words required 7 seconds to say but would scar that man for 47 years. He was finally able to make peace with his deceased dad. Be careful with words.

This also happens when we become disappointed with ourselves and say things such as "I'm are so dumb to have done that; I'm also ugly and fat and stupid," which I call "thoughtaholism." We can't seem to stop our belittling thoughts, and we spiral down to discouragement.

Second, don't take anything personally. This is especially difficult for Feeling persons who tend to take everything personally, even what they say about themselves. Just remind yourself that what people say or do reveals more about themselves than about you, the hearer.

For example, a new mother was showing off her baby to a friend who asked "What did you name her?" "Rendi," the mother replied. "Rendi?" the friend exclaimed in an unbelievable tone. "Where'd you get that weird name?"

Consequently, the new mother became very upset. In consoling her, I projected that possibly her friend had been mistreated by someone with that name. When the new mom applied the principle of not taking anything personally, she relaxed and was able to latch on to that releasing idea.

The Expectation Trap

Differences in personality underlie the bulk of interpersonal problems because we neither all require the same kind of appreciation and attention nor see what needs to be done in the same way.

As we have discussed, each personality type also has a particular style of doing things. Knowledge about temperaments equips us to perceive others' expectations and to understand our own.

The old adage "Doing what you don't like to do builds character" reflects much wisdom, but some people go too far in expecting themselves to accomplish most of the time that which exceeds their abilities, available time, physical and mental energies, or natural inclinations. This leads to self-dissatisfaction and resentment toward those who expect—or we imagine as expecting—certain performance. Eventually burnout results, so we need to be realistic about what we can honestly deliver or achieve.

Expectations of all kinds have to be identified, understood, confronted, and often rejected. Otherwise, guilt, anger, and resentment occur, and any of those emotions can be unhealthy.

Try to avoid being presumptuous. This accentuates so well what we've discussed above. Presumptions set us up for disappointment, cascading into resentment that creeps in when expectations are unfulfilled. Be what I call "kindly honest."

People who feel guilty when they realize they have not fulfilled their own or someone else's expectations must learn to recognize that a particular expectation or presumption may be unfair or inappropriate for them. The next chapter offers practical solutions for dealing with the residue of unfair expectations and guilt.

CHAPTER 5

Grappling with Guilt: Destructive Insects

Let us draw near to God with a sincere heart in full assurance of faith,
having our hearts sprinkled to cleanse us from a guilty conscience.
Hebrews 10:22

We have seen that unfulfilled expectations leave a residue of hurt feelings, irritation, and inadequacy. All these are roadblocks to effective communication, so now we will examine ways to deal with the most tell-tale effect of destructive bugs and insects in our garden: guilt and its poisonous results.

When others let us know in one way or another that we have failed to live up to their expectations by not acting a certain way or doing a particular thing, or we have fallen short of our own expectations, we are likely to be nagged and even tortured with a sense of guilt.

Especially tender targets for this poisonous emotion are those with the Feeling (Heart-Logic) preference. Tenderhearted people tend to yield more readily to others' thoughtless and unfair expectations because they hunger for harmony, want to please everyone, and are instinctively empathetic with the feelings and ideas of others. Feeling types, when asked if they struggle with guilt, respond very quickly: "Yes, all the time."

Thinking (Head-Logic) people have a certain resiliency to taking guilt trips. They certainly have to be sent there by someone else, because they rarely elect to go on their own. For example, a Thinker arriving late may be very apologetic, disappointed with her tardiness, but probably doesn't feel guilty.

"Yes, I suppose I feel guilt at times," a Thinker said, "if it's inflicted on me. If it's something I can help, I may suffer a little bit of guilt over it."

No question about it, Thinking people do experience some hint of guilt for not pleasing others, and they prefer harmony to discord. But "peace at any price" is not their motto, mainly because they do not need others' approval to function. Though Thinkers appreciate approval after they have made decisions or accomplished some project, they function well without it.

In no way do I want to give the impression that Thinkers are not caring, sensitive, helpful, or others-oriented. They are just more private about expressing or seeking affection, and their logic-based decisions protect them from assuming guilt or blame unless irrefutable facts prove otherwise.

Since Feeling people instinctively regulate what they do and say by what they think the person they want to please expects, they unconsciously set themselves up for abuse, paralleling the insidious attacks of harmful insects on the sensitive leaves, stems, and roots of plants.

Trying to speak and act according to another's whims puts the other person in control of your self-esteem. You are really saying, "I'll be your mental and physical slave if you'll give me approval."

Feeling people actually writhe in guilt when others disapprove, criticize, or blame them. Their mental anguish is devastating, even when they are innocent. This is one of the main reasons many people seek counseling.

Guilt registers an especially heavy blow when adult children blame their parents for their social or emotional problems. Mothers, especially, often experience depression after such accusations.

Unfortunately, homes that benefit one child often violate another. I've not met many people who boast of a perfect childhood. By the time most people master parenthood, their children no longer live at home. Parental guilt is a poison that doesn't just dissolve; it must be dealt with and neutralized.

Misunderstood feelings and emotions can whirl people around in endless circles. With understanding and practice, softhearted people can learn to control their emotions and alter their thinking by understanding the source and validity of their guilt trips.

The Guilt-Producing Process

Inadequacy and feelings of inferiority are two of the most destructive components of guilt. Ironically, a person may believe he is inferior simply because someone of a different personality makeup unintentionally implies it is so.

For example, without meaning to, extroverts cause feelings of inferiority to well up in introverts when they expect them to speak up or be more assertive. "Teachers always mention how quiet our children are, as though we didn't know it," Judith said. "The children are beginning to think something is really wrong with them because they are not noisy like most of the others."

On the other hand, introverts can induce feelings of inadequacy in extroverts if they fault them for their inability to speak without making errors or refer to them as "blabbermouths." Feeling-type extroverts may appear to be thick-skinned, but they are easily bruised by name calling—a cruel type of rejection used in many homes, incidentally. Feeling people are also hurt by sarcasm meant to be funny. Sarcasm roams freely in many homes, trying to mix humor with a put-down barb, but it is injurious and rarely funny. The dictionary definition is the use of irony to mock or convey contempt. Sarcasm is the source of much guilt.

Sensing people arouse iNtuitives' concept of inadequacy when they ridicule their ineptness with hands-on projects. "Why, he can't even find the hood of his car," a Sensing person may joke.

"My mother can't understand why I don't sew my children's clothes," Annie complained. "I want her to be proud of me, but I just can't get into sewing. I feel so guilty and inferior because my older sister makes all of her clothes." Many iNtuitives already struggle to compete with Sensing people's productivity—no need to rub it in!

iNtuitives can incite inferior feelings in Sensing people merely by bouncing easily from one theory to another in a discussion, or speaking in sentence fragments that hit only the high spots. "I stay away from that group," Tom said. "I'm just not on their wavelength. They lose me, and I'm afraid they're going to ask my opinion on some intellectual issue."

Many Sensing people feel generally inferior in the area of iNtuitives' analytical ability, which resembles interrogation. Since iNtuitives' natural talent for wriggling out of things often gives the false impression that they know everything, they need to avoid unintentional manipulations.

Structured people, without thinking, often imply that their sPontaneous opposites are lazy and disorganized by poking fun at them. "Haven't you finished laying your walkway yet, or are you praying for snow?" they might tease.

sPontaneous people get their licks in, too, by such tactics as sermonizing a burned-out workaholic: "You should have gone fishing with me. I told you to take time to relax." Or they might try to get a Structured person off schedule: "Come with us. You're no fun at all and are in a deep, dull rut. You'll be old before your time."

Regardless of the personality type, many parents feel inadequate when they compare their children's achievements or growth with that of others. This guilt often develops into jealousy.

What guilt are you bearing? Make your list. This is the first step in tossing it away and erasing its destructive effects.

Case Study

Guilt catches us off guard at subtle times, as softhearted Tana illustrates: "I received a call after my bedtime one Saturday evening from my friend Greta, saying, 'Tana, would you like to join my aerobics club? Our next class in on Monday night, and we meet for an hour and a half. I can get you in for half price, but I need to know right now.'

"I struggled to respond to the urgency of the call as I was waking up. Greta went on to say, 'I know you will really enjoy this, and since I am next on the list to invite a friend, I get in for half price too. But I must know now to call the teacher' and on and on. I paused a moment and then told her I would join.

"On Monday evening I reluctantly left our toddler son with my husband, who had just arrived home from a trip. I knew I would not enjoy this class for several reasons—the evening schedule, the length of the class, and the type of exercise. I prefer outdoor tennis.

"So, realizing this was not for me, I called Greta the next day to suggest that perhaps someone else would take my place and enjoy the opportunities more than I would. She became very upset with me and said, 'If you drop out, I'll look bad because one other girl I took dropped out too.'

"After saying how hurt she would be, that she would probably even cry, Greta added 'If you aren't interested in doing it for yourself, then do it for me. I am pleading with you.' What could I say? I wanted to say just count me out, but I didn't want to hurt her—so I agreed to try it again. We hung up.

"I know Greta needs me as a friend. She likes me and is depending on me to be with her in this class, but it isn't something I will enjoy. And to be very truthful, I don't get much enjoyment from this friendship. Is it my duty to continue? How far should I go? Can I learn to respect myself and my wishes first? Should I let my feeling of resentment cause the friendship to die totally, or just continue to put up with the emotional pressure?"

This type of story is repeated every day in different forms and in offices, factories, schools, churches, homes, and neighborhoods. Feeling people grapple with guilt when they don't do things others expect, yet they wrestle with resentment when they do things for people that they would rather not do.

Thinkers would respond honestly as Tana's husband did at the very beginning: "If I wasn't interested in taking aerobics, I wouldn't go—no matter who invited me or for what reasons. Friendship is not based on forcing you to do what you don't want to do."

Choosing to Feel Guilty

To be honest, we actually choose to feel guilty. People may attempt to put guilt trips on us, but the decision to feel guilty rests with us.

One summer on our way home from vacation, Jim dropped me off at my mother's house for a week—the first time I had ever visited her without my family. I was excited. He and our two youngest teenagers, who had been with us on the trip, continued on home with a loaded camper. As I envisioned their facing the monotonous challenge of unloading and putting away items from the trip (a job I usually supervised), going through the stack of mail, answering the numerous phone calls with reports from the church field, and getting the household in the swing again, I felt guilty about not being there to help.

When Jim called to let me know they had arrived safely, I confessed, "I really feel guilty about not being there." Jim's reply jolted me. "If you want to feel guilty, go right ahead," he said bluntly. "I'm perfectly happy for you to be where you are."

That was a turning point for me. I decided right then and there that if he didn't fault me for not being on hand, then feeling guilty was my own choice. So, I should forget it. I did, and I had a wonderful guilt-free visit.

Resisting Guilt

Just because you feel guilty, inferior, inadequate, or to blame doesn't mean that you really are. When you understand yourself and appreciate how you have been designed, even if people are unhappy or disappointed with you or are critical of your behavior, you can quietly say to yourself "They're not my boss." That is not egotism, but rather recognizing and preserving your self-worth.

When family, friends, or co-workers intentionally or otherwise put unfair expectations on you and you automatically take the blame or perform duties just to keep peace, the guilt you feel must be quelled at the outset if you want to keep resentment from taking root. Brenda illustrates this point with her story:

"Mother expects me to come over every Saturday afternoon. I feel anxious about it, because I know it will be a negative visit. But I feel it is something I have to do as a good daughter who is duty-bound. If I don't go, she gives me trouble.

"'My house needs vacuuming,' she'll say casually. Or 'If someone doesn't soon cut this grass, I'll have to get out there myself.' Then, for much of the time, I listen to her concerns and the faults of my siblings. What do I really want to do? Struggle with guilt? No, I must learn how to handle it, especially since much of what Mom complains about she could take care of easily by hiring it done. She's stingy with money unless she can wear or eat what it buys. And she's not nearly as tied down and mistreated as she makes it sound.

"I'm between a rock and a hard place. If I go, I resent the burden. When I think about not going, I'm overcome with not only guilt but also fear. I'm afraid that if I don't go, I'll be talked about and criticized. Somewhere through the years, as the oldest, I have accepted responsibility for protecting Mother from her problems. Or possibly I feel guilty because my husband is so sensitive to my needs and gives me plenty of space.

"Perhaps Mother is jealous of my situation. Who knows? But one thing I know is that I'm learning to ask myself questions: Is this problem mine? Can I prevent it?

Could Mom solve this if she wanted to? Am I obligated to visit my mother even though it distresses me? Is it really helping her for me to do her work?"

A statement from an earlier chapter bears repeating at this point: Insisting on harmony at any cost may be shortcutting someone else's growth in responsibility and maturity. Therefore, giving in is not always wise.

Some people have been tagged "gluttons for punishment" because in order to get attention, even abusive attention, these poor souls will bend over backward to do for people what they really don't want to do. They'll do anything to get a wee bit of approval.

That type of affection is short-lived, however. Many people suffer from "performance love," which demands rule keeping or achievements. "If you'll do such and such, I'll love you." This keeps people psychologically dependent on the "stingy" givers. Another name for this stance is conditional love.

One lover really gets the booby prize for telling his girlfriend, "If you loved me, you would be the way I want you do be."

When Thinking Pastor Jim said to his congregation, "When tenderhearted people feel a little selfish or mean, they are probably just about right," the Feeling parishioners felt exonerated.

If Feeling people never act until they feel right or good about decisions, someone's foot will no doubt be on their neck. We cannot blindly trust decisions based solely on how we feel.

Shortcutting Guilt Trips

Tana's question, "Can I learn to respect myself first?" provides the answer to all her questions. When you respect yourself, respect from others will occur naturally.

Feeling people, especially, suffer in another way: taking inappropriate blame. "I either caused these problems or could have prevented them," they reason.

"We've been married for 25 years," Gloria shared. "Every time one of our teenagers stays out too late or has any kind of problem, Phil rakes that kid over the coals but then blames me for our child's infraction. Our son questioned his dad recently about why he blames Mom for everything, and that really started an argument. Although I know I'm not a perfect wife or mother, I have questioned whether everything that goes wrong at home is my fault."

Every problem that surfaces is not one person's fault, and warmhearted people have to learn how to shield themselves from self-condemnation and choose not to have hurt feelings or guilty regrets.

I used to take the blame for every church squabble, thinking I either caused it or could have squelched it. When it became apparent to me that Jim was not devastated by discord in general, and neither was his self-esteem tied to popularity, I released myself from my false guilt. Jim taught me to ask myself a couple of questions: Is it true that I'm the cause? Am I responsible for what other people say and do?

Dealing with Mixed Emotions

When someone wants or expects you to do something you have neither the time nor inclination to do, how can you deal with the mixed emotions involved? Should you do what the other person wants, thus avoiding a confrontation in which feelings might be hurt or anger generated? Should you make an excuse to get out? How about just saying no? You must be prepared for a struggle with mixed emotions in these circumstances, especially if you've been wired to prefer Heart-Logic Feeling.

When a distasteful expectation is first presented, either ask for time to think it over (if you are not sure what you want) or tell the person right off that the answer is no. This assumes, of course, that you are not dealing with an employer or other person who has the legitimate authority to make this request of you. You may need some privacy to swish around the decision in your thinking chamber before responding, and that's okay.

But remember, if you don't say no when that's what you mean, communication becomes scrambled and resentment creeps in. If a child does not grant you consideration time and badgers you for permission, then your answer is "If you ask me one more time, the answer is no."

Some people would rather stretch the truth and tell a polite lie than risk hurting or angering someone with an honest answer. It goes something like this:

"Oh, I'm sorry," says teenage Bill who doesn't want to go to a certain party, "but my Dad has made some plans for us that I can't get out of." This indeed stretches the truth, since Bill is just planning to watch a ball game with his dad.

Bill feels he needs a more plausible explanation for Jack, believing that if he turns down the invitation outright, the tables may be turned if he wants something from Jack in the future. Besides, Bill wants to stay in good graces with the crowd in which Jack is a popular leader, so he tries a ploy quite handy for young people: using parental wishes as an "out."

Using contrived excuses—lying—makes you dislike yourself in the long run. Is it is worth disliking yourself as a person just to avoid having someone else dislike you? It's better to like the person you spend the most time with—yourself.

Learn to be honest with yourself and others. Any time you give a reason why you can't fulfill a request, check to see if it's a false reason just to protect the other person's feelings. Feeling people want the other person to think they would comply if they possibly could. But you cannot maintain popularity with everyone all the time without losing respect for yourself.

Some workers allow fellow employees to take advantage of their natural desire for harmony or friendship by doing favors. When these tenderhearted people finally wake up to the fact that others have taken advantage of their goodness—for example, willingness to work unpopular overtime slots or do the distasteful jobs—only a painful process of confrontation will change the pattern.

Maintaining Self-Esteem

- "Is it unfair to me?"
- "Will I dislike doing that?"
- "Do I want to say no?"
- "Am I being pressured?"
- "Am I trying to earn someone's approval?"
- "Do I lack respect for the person doing the asking?"

If you answer yes to most of these questions, someone may be trying to push you in a direction you don't want to go. Don't let it happen! A person tortured with guilt feelings, inadequacy, inferiority, or the tendency to always take the blame can find relief by memorizing and adopting the following guidelines:

- "I cannot please everyone all the time."
- "A request for help doesn't constitute an assignment to comply."
- "Just because several people disagree with me doesn't mean I am wrong."
- "Harmony is nice, but my efforts won't guarantee it all the time."
- "If certain others disapprove of my innate style, that's their problem."

Resolve your mixed emotions as soon as possible, so that the destructive effects on your identity and beauty are negligible. Guilt can drain the energy of your self-respect as surely as harmful insects suck life-sustaining nutrition out of plant leaves, stems, and roots.

Fighting Depression, Feelings of Inadequacy, or Discouragement

My use of the description depression relates to inadequacy or discouragement rather than the clinical definition associated with chemical imbalance. This milder form of clients' description of depression is often the result of a poor self-image, which, as we have already seen, can sometimes be caused by unrealistically appropriating feelings of guilt and inadequacy because we have failed to comply with another's expectations.

After suffering physical and mental abuse for 12 years in her first marriage, Krista's self-esteem plummeted when her new mate's family rejected her because she was a divorcee When her self-esteem was finally restored through counseling, she was able to shrug off her in-laws' narrow-mindedness as their problem, not hers. Her husband—also tenderhearted—found new confidence and contentment in standing up to his family. This once-unhappy lady has found employment and is now busy helping other troubled women to get help.

When some Feeling people are isolated from opportunities to help people, the result is often diagnosed as depression or a spiritual problem. However, this type of individual is designed to need exposure to others to function optimally. The positive feedback they receive from doing helpful things for others is their fulfillment and purpose for being a person.

If Feeling types are involved in an occupation that is not people-oriented in some way, they may suffer extreme unhappiness. Unless there is opportunity to focus on people in off hours, a change of jobs (even one with less pay) might improve their self-image.

An introverted, Sensing, tenderhearted man who preferred a scheduled lifestyle (ISFJ) worked fairly contentedly as a machinist for years, until forced overtime made it impossible to fit in his volunteer prison activities. He became very unhappy, but blamed it on spiritual weakness, midlife crisis, his mate, and so on. When a company layoff forced him to find other work, he returned to a secretarial position he had held before he was married. He has been satisfied ever since. He needed direct contact with people.

Many Thinking mates—sometimes possessive Feeling ones—disapprove of their partners' investment of fuel, time, and energy in visiting friends or volunteering their services to those in need. One man said to his mate when she wanted to reach out to a family who had suffered a house fire, "I'll tell you when and who to help. If you have time on your hands, learn to sew or do something more around the house."

This woman suffered diminished self-esteem and deep discouragement until she got involved in serving others who would respond with appreciation.

When our self-worth hinges totally on others' acceptance, opinions, and positive feedback, we are at their mercy. While there is a legitimate, instinctive need for Feeling people to locate satisfying sources of approval, there is also a need to find a healthy balance.

The latest research indicates that mild depression, or feelings of inadequacy and discouragement, can be alleviated by well-chosen behavior therapy and medication.

My own informal research bears this out. In my counseling, I suggest "walk and talk therapy." Exercise is a wonderful way to cleanse the mind and body, and talking is a natural way to unload bulging bags of depressed feelings.

In no way am I suggesting that clinical depression and the above illustrations are the same. Those suffering from clinical depression need professional medical care.

Healthy Guilt

One dictionary defines guilt as "The fact of being responsible for an offense or wrongdoing: breaking the law; remorseful awareness of having done something wrong."

Real guilt is serious business. I do not want to dilute one's responsibility for accepting appropriate blame for wrongdoing. This type of guilt cannot be explained away. Honest confession and restitution, if possible, is the only way to rid oneself of true guilt.

Many children lie because they want to avoid their parents' wrath. They find that their inner guilt about lying is easier to bear than the parental uproar and rehearsal of their infraction.

(Isn't it true that we adults also stretch or avoid the truth in order to save our reputation or admit that we are to blame?)

I like the illustration of a mother who finds her little boy's broken car behind the couch. If she asks, "Johnny, where is your new car?" she's likely to encourage Johnny into a lying "I don't know," in order to avoid a bawling-out or discipline. It is a good psychological principle not to ask questions if you know the answer. If the mother says instead, "Johnny, I found your new little car today. I'm so sorry it's broken," Johnny is likely to say, "Yeah, I tried to step on it and I was too heavy." (I learned this important principle of not asking questions when you know the answers, focusing on the problem, not attacking character, and much more from Heim Ginot's book, *Between Parent and Child*.)

Many children complain that adults do not give them time to give their side of the story. Parents can encourage truthfulness by calmly hearing the child's version and fitting the punishment to the offense. (This subject is covered in our book, *Coaching Kids*.)

Real guilt indicates the presence of sin. But John 1:9 promises: "If we confess our sins, (God) is faithful and just and will forgive us our sins and purify us from all unrighteousness." We must all learn to appreciate good, "healthy" conviction guilt, which pricks our minds when selfishness, unconcern, and falsifying emerge. As Scott Peck reminds us in *The Road Less Traveled*, we must learn to listen to our conscience.

Though I would not advocate ignoring legitimate guilt feelings, learning to consult Head-Logic will release overly sensitive people who are unhealthily controlled by false guilt. For example, even though Feeling people are naturally sensitive and make personal sacrifices easily, they are quite capable of being ugly, selfish, and unconcerned about the needs or feelings of others, especially when they have suffered much personal hurt, neglect, and rejection themselves. After therapeutic healing through positive communication that assures them of their intrinsic value and raises their self-esteem, healthy guilt can bring about a realization of their true selves.

Healthy guilt-handling for a Thinker would include the same drill while purposely considering the emotional needs and augmented sensitivity of the other 50 percent of the population.

We can learn valuable lessons from observing a flower garden. Only as we recognize the higher order of our creation "made in God's image" do we come to know our strengths and weaknesses and those of others. Then we will wisely adjust our expectations of ourselves and our fellow humans so that the best harmony can be realized.

Much heartache can be avoided if we work together to rid God's garden of the destructive insects of guilt. Like gardeners who have to recognize rascally weeds and the best way to control them to keep them from crowding and starving out plants, we will analyze next how best to deal with the weeds of resentment and disharmony that disrupt our relationships.

CHAPTER 6

Resentments: The Weeds of Disharmony

Whoever of you loves life and desires to see many good days,
keep your tongue from evil and your lips from speaking lies.
Turn from evil and do good; seek peace and pursue it.
Psalm 34:12-14

Weeds are always unwelcomed in a garden. A flower garden overtaken by weeds is a hideous sight and usually indicates gross neglect. Even a few weeds can spoil the intended beauty and harmony.

Most gardeners agree that weeds will flourish despite adverse circumstances. Most are tough, thorny, and very difficult to destroy. If left to mature, weeds ripen and yield thousands more of their highly productive seeds.

Resentments resemble weeds in many ways, sprouting when conditions are right, cropping up overnight, and surviving with no encouragement. At first, they are small and inconspicuous. Ignored, they mature and rear their ugly heads unexpectedly. In no time, resentments can destroy a beautiful life.

As with weeds, the seeds of resentment can live buried for many years before germinating. To be thoroughly destroyed, complex resentments must be dug up by the roots.

The Origin of Resentments

According to one dictionary, resentment is "a feeling of indignant displeasure at something regarded as a wrong, insult, or injury." In other words, it is a result of a real or imagined offense.

Resentments germinate mainly from unfulfilled expectations. As discussed in the previous two chapters, people sometimes resent themselves for not reaching their goals or for failing to please others. At other times, unfulfilled expectations—both assumed and spoken—that we have placed on other people sprout into resentments on both sides.

Resentments can spring from job terminations, unkept promises, oversights, passive attitudes, lack of recognition, disrespect, unfair treatment, negligence, irresponsibility, laziness, failure to assist, pushiness, presumptuous behavior, lack of understanding, and personal defaults of all kinds. The list is endless. Many deeply rooted resentments stem from long-ago emotional or physical abuse, causing mental disorders that usually require professional assistance to remove.

Weeding Out Resentments

Resentments are relatively easy to pull while they are young and tiny; they are noticed only upon close inspection. Emotional growth of the softhearted is often thwarted because they judge their worth by the way others speak to and treat them.

Tenderhearted people, for example, usually speak the way they would like to be spoken to—tenderly: "I'm sorry, but I have to disagree." Or, "I realize this is a great imposition but…"

They resent not receiving reprimands, disagreements, and directions in the same gentle manner, since otherwise they register them as put-downs.

Similarly, Feeling people also resent not being consulted in decision making, as Julie explained: "When my partner announced that he was offering our home to his teenaged niece without first asking my opinion, I was irate."

When I interviewed her mate, Dean, about this, he said: "Julie complains no matter what I do, so I decided I might as well do what I thought was right. The girl needs a home."

"Julie probably resists your decisions because she's not sure about her importance," I suggested. "Do you tell her how important she is to you—that she's number one?"

"I don't talk like that!" he stormed. "In fact, we can't seem to talk."

"Unless you acknowledge her style of listening and learn to speak her language, you'll have two crises on your hands," I said. "If Julie feels manipulated and taken for granted, she'll not be willing to help your niece, which may likely intensify problems for all concerned."

Many weeks later, Julie expressed some honest evaluations and mature solutions in a letter to her husband:

"Dear Dean: Do you see how my keeping my thoughts inside angered you? This is how I feel when I discover your hidden 'I resents.' Why can't we expose these resentments as they develop and avoid the two-hour potluck? I want to encourage you to become the best person you can become. I want you to encourage me to become the best person I can become. I long to be totally honest. I yearn for you to be the same.

"I will remove my expectations of wanting to be verbally affirmed. When it happens, it will be a bonus. When I feel you are allowing situations to supersede my importance, I'll try to deal tactfully with it. Let's start over."

Typically, old hurts can't be solved easily nor even recalled properly. Many resentments, especially those originating in the home, appear trivial to bystanders, but these little weeds quickly grow into big ones if they are ignored. After many years of growth, they will have to be painfully dug out by the roots, like onion grass, since plowing under does not destroy their seeds of disharmony.

Eliminating Young Resentments in the Home

"Alice is not keeping her end of the bargain," Ryan ranted. "Our house just doesn't look like a home—not a plant in sight. My mom had plants in every room."

Saying "I do" does not automatically endow a partner with a green thumb, any more than it equips a mate to repair the washing machine. Ryan's expectations are unfair.

"What are you going to cook for my parents, Bonnie?"

"I've told you, John, that I can't cook. You've certainly observed that over the last few months. I've done nothing to indicate that I would ever be able to cook," she defended.

"You're a woman! Some little part of me still secretly hoped you could cook," he pouted.

Some iNtuitive women neither like to cook nor enjoy taking care of plants. Many resent cleaning a house and washing clothes. Since they prefer analytical involvements, they often enjoy rearing children, which involves future planning and different kinds of growth—psychological, emotional, spiritual, and physical.

In a home, an individual's expectations must be analyzed carefully and blended with the personalities of family members.

A mother who works outside the home may resent other members of the family for not helping with household chores. In my own experience I like to be in charge of the house until time pressures intervene. Then I expect help, especially if someone is merely watching TV or reading a magazine. I have accepted housecleaning as my responsibility since I elected to get married and have children. Even though I'm an iNtuitive, I actually enjoy housework. But cleaning the bathtub is one job I dislike, so I have tried to dump this chore.

After our son moved back home after college, I mentioned several times that the tub needed to be cleaned, that I didn't have time to clean it, and that he helped dirty it. Because I dislike the job and because he pays room and board, I felt a bit guilty about trying to slough it off on him, so I hoped he would volunteer out of sympathy for me. My effort was useless. Thinkers (like our son) are fairly guilt-trip immune.

I put the Ajax can and the cleaning cloth on the tub. No luck. Once I sprinkled the cleansing powder in the tub before he showered, but he didn't take that hint either. But my assumption that I deserved this kind of assistance without asking created the right expectation-condition for resentment to build up. I didn't want to resent him, so I applied two helpful rules: mentally acknowledge the expectation (or resentment), and substitute a verbalized request (or desire) for the unspoken or unclear expectation. It went like this:

"I'd like for you to take a couple of minutes to clean the tub this morning." This provided him with a choice—yes or no. I could learn immediately what his response would be rather than wonder if he caught the hint.

"No problem," he replied. As easy as that. Was I ever impressed! If he had said no, we could have had reason for a family conference. A person who respects and loves you will want you to be satisfied. If your requests are unreasonable, it's better to get that out in the open.

I have discovered that resentment revolves around things one usually dislikes doing and/or is expected to do. Many parents feel guilty if they fail to meet the physical and emotional needs of their family, especially if they are single parents. People can even feel guilty for feeling guilty! On top of that, the guilt may be tinged with resentment when they receive no positive responses from their children, who are often too young or immature to appreciate sacrifices made for them.

"I used to make meals and other things to get approval from my family," Anne confessed. "But when they didn't come through with appreciation and a little assistance, I was filled with resentment and self-pity. I hate resenting the people I love the most," she sighed.

Anne did not realize that it is unfair to expect a mate or child to be thoughtful in the same areas and ways that she was. But anyone can learn to be sensitive to specific needs once they understand how important it is to a person they care about.

After Anne pinpointed the source of her resentment and expressed her expectations to herself, she reported:

"I decided that doing my duties because I 'wanted to' would bypass my resentment build-up. I have discovered that when I don't expect appreciation, and then do receive affirmation, it's a gift. My resentment toward my family has subsided greatly, now that I don't expect something they won't or don't know how to give. I feel much better."

Most family members are unaware how they take their moms and dads for granted; they need to be reminded from time to time that appreciation is in vogue. It's even alright for a mom to say, "I'm making breakfast because I want to, but I could surely use some applause about now!"

A mate may resent her tenderhearted partner's tendency to let his boss and relatives push him around and take advantage of his need for harmony. But a bossy mate creates a fertile ground for resentment to grow in him and in the children who are listening. (Tenderheartedness will be discussed more fully in chapter 8.)

Sometimes parents resent a child for deeper reasons, as Claudia shared:

"My husband and I are separated. Our daughter, Lisa, blames me for her father's inability to present a firm backbone for this family. I have accepted all her accusations because I feel very inadequate, as well as wanting to keep peace—even if it means taking the blame for something that's not totally my fault.

"However, when I see Lisa walking up the driveway with our granddaughter, Suzie, expecting me to drop everything and babysit, I actually seethe with resentment. All she wants is what I can do for her. She cares nothing about how much she imposes or what kind of mess her child makes in my house or whether I'm tired."

Acknowledging the Situation

In the example above, I counseled Claudia to apply the twofold approach I had used with my son in the tub-scrubbing incident: Acknowledge the source of resentment mentally. "Lisa expects me to take the blame for our separation. I am not responsible for her father's actions and inabilities. Lisa expects me to take care of Suzie without forewarning. She expects me to meet her needs but cares nothing about mine."

Then, verbalize the expectation. "Lisa, I would prefer to keep Suzie when I know ahead of time, rather than any time you choose." This declaration calls for a response from Lisa. They will both need to communicate about reasonable expectations. Claudia might start off by saying, "Are you aware that I also hurt over this separation and expect a little kindness, support, and consideration from you?" An answer is requested.

The "Ruthism," as my clients refer to the principle of acknowledging the situation, is 50 percent of the solution and works wonders.

In the Office

In an office where workers share duties, resentment often runs rampant as each expects the others to do those jobs no one likes to do. Jenny had this to say:

"The other gals assume I like to answer the phone, but I answer it just because I can't stand to hear it ring and I don't want the boss to bawl us out. They also just walk out at the end of the day as though I'm supposed to lock up everything, clean out the coffee pot, and turn off the machines. I guess I have just chosen to do these jobs to keep peace, but inside I'm burning.

"Even though our boss has never told me to do all those extra jobs, I just accepted doing them without complaint. To stop doing them now would probably cause some friction within the office. My co-workers suppose I am only doing those things because I enjoy it, but I really have deep resentment toward them all."

Jenny needs to apply the second part of our rule—verbalize the expectations—so she might tell her coworkers: "Answering the phone is not just my responsibility, so I would like one of you to answer it, too. And I want us to take turns locking up, cleaning up, and turning off machines."

The others' responses to each of these statements will provide opportunity for good communication and clearing the air. If not, the boss certainly needs to set some guidelines.

Of course, turning expectations into requests could be answered with "I don't care what you want" or "I can't deliver what you request." There are risks involved in being honest. But I would rather know, for instance, that our son doesn't care how I feel about cleaning the tub and that he never intends to clean it than to keep hoping that sometime he will appreciate me enough to do it without being asked.

In the Community

Monica was ecstatic about having an entire week to herself—the first time in her 13 years as a mother. The youngest child, Jennifer, was finally old enough to join her brother and sister for the YMCA day camp. Monica was pleased with her ability to make such a big decision without the help of her husband. But then Mrs. Strong called about the opportunity to be a counselor, promising that "your children would get to go free." That didn't really influence Monica, but she was filled with parental guilt when Mrs. Strong said, "Most parents don't realize how much they miss by not being with their children in such a creative outdoor atmosphere. And we are desperate for help."

"There's no reason why I couldn't go," Monica reasoned aloud. "I really didn't have anything definite planned except to read and do some writing and maybe shop alone. It's selfish of me to want a whole week without my children," she thought, which raised her guilt level by several decibels. "And I just might miss something important to my children," she further counseled herself.

"I need to know your decision right away," Mrs. Strong coaxed.

"Okay, I'll do it," Monica said. "As soon as I hung up," Monica told me later, "I knew I had made the wrong decision, but I had been trying to make cognitive decisions and stick with them, so I figured this was one I'd have to stick to.

"I dreaded each day at camp. I was bored and kept thinking about how much I'd looked forward to my private time. I made the most of the week by enjoying the outdoors and getting acquainted with the other counselors and leaders. But I still regret letting Mrs. Strong talk me into something I really didn't want to do. I don't know if I resent myself or Mrs. Strong the most. It's my Feeling nature in charge of me again," she analyzed correctly. "How can I control this tendency?"

Those who base their decisions on feelings are most often guilty of saying yes when they mean no. As previously mentioned, they are wise to make a pact with themselves to say automatically, "I need time to think it over," to anyone who wants them to be on a committee, teach a class, donate a day, be in a club, or volunteer to do anything. If the other person presses for an immediate answer, let it be "No."

As you later consider the request, first ask yourself: "Is this something I really want to do?" Then apply the technique of a Thinking decision maker by writing down the pros and cons of doing or not doing it. As you expose new facts and possibilities, run the options through a Thinker's head if this is feasible.

Meeting thorny resentments head-on takes courage, especially for Heart-Logic people, who want to be helpful and need approval from those around them. The positive side is that disagreements provide material for discussion. Solving little problems forms invisible bonds between people of all temperaments.

Unfulfilled expectations, which create the climate for the weeds of resentment to grow, look very harmless in their infancy, but unless we conscientiously and consistently remove these young sprouts, our garden's beauty will be at great risk.

Yanking Out Mature Resentments

Resentments with a few years' growth are not so easily eliminated. They must be yanked out forcibly, though taking action at this juncture will likely disturb other plants around them. That's a risk we must take if we envision a healthy garden.

Marcia tells of her longstanding resentment, which centers on her in-laws' expectations:

"My husband's father lives with us. We're the only ones who still reside in his hometown. This works okay until the holidays when Wayne's brothers and their families descend on us from out of town to visit Grandpa. Then my resentment really builds up.

"Every one of our holidays is pre-planned. I'm cooking, cleaning, and crowding up rather than spending the vacation time with our children.

"I'm an elementary school teacher. We rarely are free to do what our immediate family would enjoy. I resent terribly not being able to establish our own family tradition with our four children, who are fast approaching high school. Wayne feels the same way I do, but we don't know how we can swing private time with all his family here. We'd love to celebrate Christmas with just our children, or sometimes with my family.

"We've considered going out to eat, but then I would feel guilty about not hosting. Besides that, Wayne's family wouldn't understand and would be hurt, which would give us another problem to solve. Wayne just does not have the courage to confront his family, but we agree something has to be done.

"We've hinted about having Christmas somewhere else, but we really don't want to leave home, especially since we're the only ones with young children. I don't know why they don't invite their father to their homes. They've all had children, so they should know how important spending time with them is. But they've done this now for several years, and I don't think it's a rut they want to leave. We're trapped."

Family expectations hold millions in their silent grip. The resentment they activate can grow like a blight, ultimately disfiguring or destroying healthy relationships.

"Which do you think is more detrimental," I asked Marcia, "your resentment or their hurt? You are not only upset with them because they come, but you also are disappointed with yourself for not having the courage to schedule your own family time. So, you end up with two mads.

"Wayne's relatives have their private family time all the other weeks of the year. You are never alone, unless you purposely plan things away from home. His family has placed expectations on you to be present because they have no idea that you'd rather do something else.

"Resentment ends in defeat, so what you're piling up will eventually surface and produce a big hurt. It's better to remove resentments while they're manageable than to undergo a major upheaval. When something unexpected or undesirable happens, a willingness to confront exactly what you're feeling gives you some measure of control."

"But I'd feel guilty if it hurt anyone's feelings," Marcia predicted.

"Would you rather ignore the problem and feel resentful or guilty but be working toward a solution? Doing the right thing doesn't always feel right."

"You're right: I've got to face the music. Oh, I hate confrontation with a passion," she moaned.

"Yes, you probably will suffer from guilt, but you must tell yourself the truth—that having a private family affair, the desire of your heart, is not sinful.

"Just because you feel guilty doesn't mean you necessarily are. Make sure your intentions are noble. You are not trying to avoid people or shirk your duty; you're just attempting to establish family traditions the way you and Wayne envision them.

"If you let the years tick away much longer and never satisfy your desire or fulfill your needs, the roots of your resentment toward your father-in-law and perhaps Wayne and his entire family will extend even deeper.

"Begin looking for the positives in this event. Make a commitment to meet the challenge in a way that makes you a stronger person. It takes a disciplined effort to learn to say, 'It's up to me to make something good come out of this.' Maybe the out-of-town family would enjoy having Grandpa visit them if they only knew you wouldn't mind sharing him at holidays.

"Wayne's family may even feel that you monopolize Grandpa. They may also assume that you approve of the family tradition of coming to your house.

"In any case, Wayne should not only be present for the discussion, but he should also lead it. His family would no doubt accept his opinions with less resentment than they would yours."

Airing their difficulties was not as painful as Marcia had anticipated. When Wayne's brothers and sisters heard the facts, they were quite willing to make adjustments. Each family has chosen a holiday to share with Grandpa, who really enjoys a change of scenery. Marcia and Wayne have even more freedom than they had hoped.

These same principles can be applied to the office, school, community, and church. Old resentments will not go away without a weeding effort. It may be helpful at this point to mention that Structured people are usually more willing than their sPontaneous counterparts to plod through problems step by step.

Many Sensing-Feeling-Spontaneous people practice the ostrich method of sticking their heads in the sand and expecting the problems to disappear, but they don't—they just spread.

iNtuitives are generally more likely to tackle relationship problems, because past failures do not discourage them. But Feeling-iNtuitives may avoid confrontations as long as possible since they do not like to disrupt "harmony," which to them means the absence of argument.

We know that silence is no guarantee that harmony is present. It's better to cause a little trouble to clear up resentments when they start than to allow a blight of destructive uncontrolled growth.

Uprooting Ancient Resentments

Molly, a young mother of two, harbored a resentment so filled with pain that she buried its memory deeply and had never told anyone about it. Her father had told her as a child that she was God's gift to him and that she should never reveal their secrets.

This father sexually abused his daughter for years before she realized what was happening. When Molly finally understood that it was wrong and began resisting his overtures, he would force her into compliance.

When she threatened to tell her mother, he countered with "I'll leave. Who'll take care of your brothers and sisters then?" Guilt and fear gripped her for three years.

(At the same time her dad was taking advantage of Molly, he was being honored as "Father of the Year" by his church. Yes, this is a true story.)

Molly finally left home by getting married. But she worried about her younger sisters, especially since she had never told anyone about her father—not even her mother. (Records show that most mates deny that incestuous abuse could be true and choose to reject the daughter.) Molly hoped she could forget what happened to her, but instead her resentment toward her father intensified.

Several years elapsed. Though Molly avoided her father as much as possible, guilt, fear, and resentment were taking their toll on her. Molly's relationship with her husband was adversely affected. And now that they had a baby girl, Molly was not comfortable bringing the child around her grandfather. Fear for her daughter's well-being is what brought Molly for professional help, which was also needed to heal her own emotional wounds.

Many mothers voice this concern. Oftentimes it involves fear of a brother, friend, or uncle. Sexual abuse is one of the most serious problems a gal or guy faces, and it has to be dealt with. Molly should share her information with her sisters and mother in order to protect the younger girls. Of course, any person who physically abuses a child needs psychological counseling. No doubt, her father is a victim to his own deep-rooted resentments and unfulfilled expectations, which also cry for professional attention.

Uprooting this fearful resentment will certainly create problems for the entire family. But in the long run it will eliminate much of its deep-seated pain and prevent worse consequences in the future. Such ancient resentments have to be carefully dug out by their well-established roots, as the following story also illustrates:

Joel was born to Shirley while she was in high school, and her mother made sure that Shirley suffered emotionally for getting pregnant. Shirley had unsuccessfully attempted to gain her mother's approval since childhood, but her unfulfilled expectations kept Shirley's self-esteem at zero.

Shirley finally moved out on her own, accepting the struggles of single parenting. For years she worked long, exhausting hours doing jobs that didn't interest her but that supplied a paycheck to support Joel and herself.

At least her son would appreciate and approve of her, she reasoned. However, even that expectation backfired when Joel moved out the day after he graduated from high school. Shirley had expected that out of gratitude for all she had sacrificed for her son, as an adult he would stay and gladly take care of her.

Joel's top priority was obviously not his mother's welfare. Often a parent like Shirley is filled with resentment toward anyone who receives her child's affection and attention (which is most often the child's partner). In her case, the pain went deeper, since she had years ago been disappointed by her own parent.

Expecting grown children to stick around to offer financial and physical support and company is a source of great disappointment for conditional-love parents. Young people expect that they have earned the freedom to launch out on their own pursuits and enter their private world of relationships.

Parents are better advised to look way ahead, anticipate the time when their children will probably leave, and encourage them to be independent, even though that means being left alone. A parent's sacrificial years with a child should not create an expectation that obligates the child.

Naomi's story provides one more illustration and a solution:

"My mother has made all my decisions since I was a child. She chose my hairstyle, my friends, my school courses, my clothing, my summer jobs—everything. If I ever disagreed with her opinion, she knew how to put a guilt trip on me. My, the guilt!

"Mother wanted me to equate her authority with God's. Down deep I knew I should insist on making some of my own decisions, but no one at our house crossed Mom—not even our father. He just sat back quietly and let her have control. My way of rebelling was to marry someone she did not approve of. I didn't really approve of Murray, either, but it felt good to go against my mother's wishes for once. I also wanted an excuse to leave home.

"I have paid for my mistake many times over. My biggest problem now is a horrible marriage. But I still detest my mother's trying to dictate my decisions. I hate myself for being pushed around."

Like Naomi, many people reject themselves if they feel rejected by someone they love. But Naomi also harbored a strong case of resentment against her mother. Being honest was difficult for Naomi because the unjustified guilt she felt for not receiving her mother's approval was a difficult pill to swallow.

Holding long-term resentment means you have given that other person control of your emotional state. Naomi had never learned that her self-image was as important as recognizing the worth of others. Naomi would never recover her self-esteem until she got rid of the burden of her resentment.

Naomi had waited expectantly for years for her mother to improve and become what she wanted in a parent. She now knew that there was no way to change her mother. Her mother was "real" the way she was. Like many other introverts, especially if they are iNtuitives and Spontaneous problem solvers, Naomi had tried to change the situation by avoiding a confrontation. She had curtailed visits with her mother, but that injured her father and her children and failed to get at the root of the problem. The only option left was to change her own attitude, which meant forgiving her mother.

Naomi did not want to confront her mother with a lifetime list of resentments that her mother would probably deny anyway, so she rehearsed her resentments to an empty chair in which she envisioned her mother sitting.

"My mother has changed," Naomi announced at our next session.

"Have you talked with her in person about your resentments?" I questioned.

"No, I haven't. That's what's so weird," she said. "Mom doesn't know anything about that list. I saw her briefly the other night. For once she asked no questions but told my grandparents that she has confidence in whatever decision I'm going to make regarding my marriage.

"But best of all, I feel at peace for the first time in years. I have recently learned that my mother disappointed her mother when she got married. She's had problems similar to mine without my knowing it. She was trying to force me to avoid the same problems she had as a young girl. I have to appreciate her for that," Naomi said with a heavy sigh.

To keep her resentments under control, Naomi should do only those things that she wants to do, even if her mother suggests otherwise. Honestly acknowledging her differences in opinion with her mother will also ward off new resentments.

Being honest despite the possibility that others may disapprove, be disappointed, or even outraged is far better than cultivating resentments. Again, acknowledging a situation is 50 percent of the solution.

Naomi accepted her mother as she was and did not expect change. She could understand why they had differences once she learned that she herself was an Introverted-iNtuitive-Spontaneous person while her mother, an extrovert who was also Sensing and highly Structured, was very rule-oriented.

Naomi has also lowered her expectations to those her mother could fulfill and has learned to verbally disagree with her mother. Now, though she never expects her mother to agree with her or compliment her on anything, when her mother does bestow approval, Naomi considers it an extra treat.

Lower your expectations of those people who are evidently not temperamentally capable of acting maturely or unselfishly by your standards. Some very nice people are insensitive to others' feelings, need for approval, or lifestyle. Being honest in verbalizing what you want to do or have happen is part of effective communication, which is serious business and not always pleasant, especially at the outset. Have you ever heard that anger is our friend? The next chapter discusses the benefits of cultivating healthy expressed anger in sweetening relationships.

CHAPTER 7

Constructive Anger: Protective Spraying

A fool shows his annoyance at once,
but a prudent man overlooks an insult.
Proverbs 12:16

In your anger do not sin; when you are on your beds,
search your hearts and be silent.
Psalm 4:4

Anger, when properly understood and controlled, can be a helpful emotion that is beneficial to relationships, just as sprays are handy remedies for controlling the insects that chomp on the leaves and stems of plants or the pesky weeds that slowly strangle tender root systems.

When sprayed or dusted with the right formula, a garden's beauty and health can be preserved and enhanced. Inappropriate chemicals or using them at the wrong time or in incorrect proportions can injure the very plants we wish to protect.

Expressions of anger are as varied as the weeds and injurious insects that must be controlled if our garden is to thrive. Because feelings of anger and how to utilize them constructively are so widely misunderstood and unappreciated, proper attention must be directed to this powerful emotion.

Uncontrolled or stored anger causes fears, guilt, embarrassment, hurt, anxieties, or disappointments. Any of these feelings can result in resentment, which is always self-defeating.

Our basic goal should be to neutralize or prevent common resentments. Developing a positive approach toward anger and learning how to use it properly will accomplish this, since angry feelings slow down our productivity and cloud our thinking. Most of all, out-of-control anger inhibits effective communication.

Misused anger is a giant wrecking ball. It smashes relationships and spreads havoc in the lives of the innocent and the offender. The results of misdirected anger are especially deadly when they injure the people we love the most.

The presence of anger is often a subtle surpriser, surfacing when one least expects it or when time to settle an issue is at a premium. Angry feelings need to be carefully analyzed and followed to their source, but first we need a definition.

One dictionary says that anger is "a feeling of extreme displeasure, hostility, indignation, or exasperation toward someone or something: rage; wrath; ire."

Anger is a general term used to denote temporary displeasure and may have no outward expression. Rage and fury imply intense, uncontained, explosive emotion. Fury can be very destructive, and rage more justified by circumstances. Ire is a poetic term for anger, while resentment refers to the ill will and suppressed anger generated by a sense of grievance. One feels indignation at seeing the mistreatment of someone or something dear and worthy.

How much do you really understand about anger? Take the following quiz by circling T (True) or F (False) for each statement. Check your answers by referring to the key below the quiz.

F	1.	The more you love someone, the less you will get angry with that person.	T
F	2.	Lack of anger and patience are the same.	T
F	3.	Anger is sin.	T
F	4.	Anger is a God-given release.	T
F	5.	Verbally expressing anger is wrong.	T
F	6.	Unexpressed anger can make you ill.	T
F	7.	People express anger in different ways.	T
F	8.	A person chooses whether to be angry.	T
F	9.	Anger is handled best when ignored.	T
F	10.	Some people never get angry.	T
F	11.	Lack of anger could indicate lack of love for the person who has offended you.	T
F	12.	Letting anger out gradually is better than holding it in.	T

(False: 1, 2, 3, 5, 9, 10; True: 4, 6, 7, 8, 11, 12)

The Sources and Functions of Anger

Many people deny that they have angry feelings because they believe that anger is unspiritual and a sign of immaturity or weakness. Others assume that an aggressive display of temper is the only way anger is expressed or experienced. But anger is evoked when any person or thing hinders our forward progress, challenges our intelligence, or takes us for granted. In short, we become angry when we are treated with disrespect. Here are a few common examples:

- Parents' anger is aroused when kids sass them, show disrespect, or leave trails of belongings.
- Grandparents' anger erupts when children lack respect for them and their authority.
- Teachers exhibit anger when students disrupt their class.
- Truckers boil when a slow-moving motorist pulls in front of them on a steep downgrade.
- Children seethe when not allowed to tell their side of the story.
- Bosses fume when workers cannot get along or time is wasted.
- Partners object to being neglected or taken for granted.
- Mates are offended when not consulted on family decisions.
- Lovers' anger is expressed in jealousies.

Anger is functional—a facilitator—appearing in all sorts of styles to alert, warn, or announce existing or approaching problems. A surge of anger is merely a warning that trouble is lurking or already upon us—similar to environmental warnings such as the nagging screech of an alarm; annoying beepers that summon; buzzers signaling an unbalanced laundry load; whistles, sirens, bells, yells, screams, cries; fire and burglar alarms; the ding-ding-ding at railroad crossings; the silent warnings of blinking lights; the flapping of high-wind pennants; or the signaling of waving flags. Immediate attention is critical for making adjustments that will prevent problems, surmount obstacles, or avoid disaster.

Although warnings are annoying, they have a good purpose. Many people either avoid warning signals until they become insensitive to them, or else they become embroiled with the signals themselves, rather than giving attention to the conditions that triggered the alert.

It can be risky business to ignore or deal impulsively with feelings of anger. In either case, personal relationships are sure to suffer. Conversely, if anger pinpoints the source of the problem by initiating in-depth communication, sturdy bonds of friendship and love are most likely to develop.

Check the following list to see how many potential sources of anger you perceive in others or regularly experience yourself:

- strong disagreement with roommates or housemates, including one's family
- anguish of inferiority feelings
- hurt from false accusations and put-downs
- distress when taken for granted
- disappointment
- anxiety stemming from loneliness

- guilt from disagreement with and/or disappointing others
- discouragement with personal failures and lack of initiative
- jealousy and envy of those who receive abundantly or achieve much
- pain from neglect
- trauma of physical or mental abuse
- dissatisfaction with personal appearance or abilities
- losing an important game
- being laughed at for something you can't control

Many people deny that they ever succumb to feelings of anger. Just as many believe that putting their head in the sand or turning a deaf ear to unpleasantness erases the emotion and eliminates the need for resolving the problem. Wrong both times! Angers do not dissolve or dissipate automatically. They either fester from neglect or are acknowledged and handled constructively.

Identifying Anger

Common indications that angry feelings are being expressed include the following behavior symptoms. Place a check by your favorites, but please don't assume that whenever these problems occur—especially the last six items—that angry feelings are definitely the cause.

grit teeth	break something	stick out tongue
run away	spit	have clammy hands
bite nails	bite	blush
kick	scream	pout
punch	stomp feet	have muscle aches
lie	slam door	have a headache
cry	curse	get sleepy
pull hair	name-call	experience insomnia
throw things	make an obscene gesture	perspire profusely
seethe silently	clean or shake fist	have nausea

Though reading over the list at this calm time may be rather amusing, these expressions can serve as important warnings—"red flags," I call them—that an existing or potential problem is threatening our self-esteem or relationship with another person. Unless we give proper attention to anger signals, we will store such a crop of cautions that either we will be overwhelmed and overtaken by their effect or become numbed and insensitive to their message.

When we learn to identify our personal anger signs, whether expressed in explosive outbursts or felt in silent misery, we will better understand ourselves and be able to avoid immature behavior. Ignoring anger never solves anything.

Appreciating Anger

Many strange ideas about feelings of anger exist. For example, some people assume that a certain threshold of distress tolerance is present in one's genetic makeup; thus, the inability to cope with problems calmly (or at all) is inherited: "I explode because my dad does." "Fury is a family trait." This theory would also imply that it is impossible to change one's reactions and responses permanently.

While there may not be a clear-cut case for a genetic explanation of one's anger threshold, understanding the different personalities sheds much light on why and how individuals respond and react to stresses. Generally, extroverts will be verbal when pressured, while introverts will more likely retreat. Structured people want things settled immediately, especially if they are also Thinkers. But if they are Feelers, they will no doubt want someone to accompany them in working through the situation.

Tenderhearted people seem to experience the majority of relationship difficulties because they have difficulty functioning without acceptance and harmony. sPontaneous people seem to have the shortest fuses and are more likely to resort to an immediate fight-or-flight technique.

Understand that every personality, if put under enough stress, is capable of running or fighting, whether the latter recourse be with mouth, fists, or pen. (Several of my clients have shared some stinging letters of angry rebuke they have had to work through.) We would all be wise not only to appreciate the particular tendencies of each personality preference but also endeavor to develop the areas of our own least preferred behavior for better balance.

The few people who believe that admitting anger is nonspiritual, immature, weak, or totally negative often attempt to conceal their feelings in order to gain both self-respect and the approval of others. Ironically, though, heaping guilt on oneself because of anger produces more subtle hostility. Ignored angers eventually take their toll mentally and physically.

Some people mistakenly assume that resignation and passivity are the opposites of anger and thus more acceptable. Others, who cannot silence their feelings, fault themselves for their defensive fly-off-the-handle tendencies. Both of these attitudes are shortsighted and can be dangerously deceptive. Anger itself is neither wrong nor negative. It is simply an attitude, a legitimate feeling that gauges something deep inside. How one expresses and handles the emotion is the important consideration.

Since so many people assume that admitting anger means acknowledging their own selfishness, conceit, or weakness, and that showing anger indicates a lack of forgiveness and a moral failure, they may miss the true value of anger as a relational tool.

Anger—what calls it forth and how we acknowledge its existence—is a remarkable revealer of true character. It exposes both commendable and selfish traits, both good and poor values. Truly, how we handle an emotional crisis shows our real self.

A person might plead in embarrassment, "How can I get rid of my temper?" The answer is that you can't, nor would you want to! Anger is here to stay. Anger is actually a gift to keep us from exploding. Without anger we would be spineless, unmotivated, and uninteresting.

Managing Anger

Anger, like love, is a feeling everyone struggles to understand, but the mark of maturity is proven by the way angry feelings are handled. There seem to be two basic immature responses to anger: noisy overreaction or stony silence. Depending on your personality makeup, your expression of anger usually will be either straightforward or disguised. Both are deadly if not appreciated and handled constructively.

Spontaneous and Impulsive Anger

Noisy and showy and often evidenced in arguments and sometimes black eyes, spontaneous and impulsive anger is the most common or best-known anger response. It also requires the least amount of thought. Some people pop off like firecrackers, curtly speak their minds, or jump to some handy defense with little thought concerning their listener.

Sharp-tongued, outspoken people do benefit somewhat from the pop-off-valve emotional release that comes from venting their feelings, but their relief is often at the expense of others' injured emotions and bodies. Many people who react this way dislike themselves afterwards, whereas timid people—the sometimes-shy extroverts or reserved introverts—may observe the confidence and courage shown and wish they could stand up and likewise unload what's on their mind.

Since uncontrolled anger of any kind wrecks friendships and confuses issues, outgoing and sPontaneous extroverts—who seem to wrestle most with this noisy, impulsive expression of feeling—need to learn how to activate the cooling-down system and generate good results.

Ignored or Simmering Anger

Common, too, but rarely called anger are the hurt feelings that result from another's steamrolling. This is basically injured pride, a malady primarily of Feeling people. Patience and endurance of mistreatment are not synonymous with lack of anger. The proverbial "cold shoulder" is fueled by simmering, silent resentments.

A few people even boast that they have no temper, but this is only because they lack the courage to admit when something or someone distresses them. People with low self-esteem suffer most with this type of inner anger. Smoldering resentments, more commonly referred to as bearing grudges, drag a person to almost a complete stop, demolishing self-confidence in their wake.

Unfortunately, many spiritual people ignorantly regard the endurance of unfair criticism or personal neglect as a high goal of a believer, as though such treatment can be equaled with humility. Some even permit physical abuse under this guise. Sorry, but such grievances are most often byproducts of poor communication, lack of respect, and emotional abuse.

Angry feelings cannot be ignored or covered up forever. Leave a splinter in your finger and the skin may heal over it, but annoying pain or a deep-seated infection will be a constant reminder. If you extract the splinter promptly and gently, the wound may bleed and ache, but healing will come.

The resentments resulting from ignored anger work like a cancer, eating away at the roots of stability and causing illness, anxiety, depression, sleeplessness, digestive problems, or serious emotional disorder—as verified by health providers.

Sometimes silent sufferers allow hurts to simmer and smolder in destructive resentment until the anger circuit becomes overloaded and finally explodes over some minor mishap in a nerve-shattering bombshell. This can subject both givers and receivers of the angry tirade to mental and often physical injury.

Is Anger Sin?

Many religious groups preach that anger is sin. This is not the case. Uncontrolled anger can lead to sin, but anger itself is a reminder—a helper. The apostle Paul tell us, "In your anger do not sin" (Eph. 4:26). In scanning the Gospels, one will discover that Jesus was angry often. Yet, he was totally sinless.

Anger is not evil. It is a God-instilled survival emotion. All human emotions are divine in origin, given to us for our protection, since God wants us to survive. However, the misuse of anger is evil. We have a right to our feelings nonetheless.

Allowing any feeling to influence us toward evil thoughts and actions is wrong. Mishandled anger is the root of many broken relationships and sinful acts. Since Jesus experienced anger many times, there is evidently nothing wrong with feeling or acknowledging angry emotions. However, Jesus' anger was always on the behalf of others rather than for his own defense, thus revealing his holy character. That's love in action—peacemaking.

Our feelings and opinions are legitimate but the tone, body language, and content determine if our communication hurts or helps.

Anger toward emotional hurts stemming from the lack of communication that results in broken homes and relationships causes people-oriented workers such as myself to dedicate every possible minute to counseling, writing, and speaking.

Balancing Expectations

Sometimes, in our idealism—and occasionally in our hostility and cynicism—we build up false pictures of other persons and of situations we expect to encounter. Then, if the persons and situations are not what we anticipated, we have problems coping with the unexpected reality. Unfortunately, most people don't know how to benefit from the signs of anger that precede the resentments that inevitably arise when our expectations are unfulfilled.

Often, relationships break up because two immature people build up false images of each other, expecting the other to act and talk as they prescribe and often unfairly demand. Anger prevails until expectations can be identified and reasonably considered.

When the reality of a mate's humanity is discovered, both partners may be stunned. Similarly, without realizing it, parents often contribute to the unreal images their children have of them. Then, when children discover that their parents have human weaknesses and inabilities, they are disillusioned and feel angry. Resentments sneak in easily in such situations.

Profiting from Anger

Since unsettled hurts emerge as resentment, then expand to bitterness and hostility, and finally grow to hatred, we need to recognize and deal constructively with these obstacles as they arise. No one is immune to angry feelings or expert at self-control, but it is possible to learn how to express our feelings positively, no matter how Extroverted or Introverted, iNtuitive or Sensing, Feeling or Thinking, sPontaneous or Structured we may be.

If you are a reserved person, learn to identify, accept, and admit openly any angry feelings. Perhaps you have a sensitive friend who will gladly listen while you verbalize your innermost feelings.

If you are prone to speak too heatedly, too quickly and foolishly, practice delaying your retorts for an hour or two. Use your adrenaline surge in cleaning, running, exercising, or something more constructive. Think completely through your statements before speaking. Write them out or share them with a trusted friend.

We can see ourselves as we really are by looking at the way we react to an oversight, a put-down, an accusation, a disagreement, manipulation, or some good deed we have done that no one acknowledges. Remember that crisis reveals character. As a negative person or experience enters your life, regard your emotional reaction as an opportunity to polish the particular area that has been exposed by your responses.

Conflict can be a friend in disguise. As you study your responses, you will see your character in technicolor. You can then refine and work on the revealed immature or weak areas.

Anger and Honesty

Sometimes empty conversation can be a means of evading the real issues. When this occurs, communication is not genuine but merely gamesmanship. We are wearing masks and denying anger signals if we cover up the truth or say one thing when we really mean another. Theodore Isaac Rubin, M.D., says in *The Angry Book* that feeling anger is like feeling hunger, loneliness, love, and fatigue. Anger reveals our personal needs and crossed values. Ignoring the feeling does nothing to meet the needs exposed.

Edna lamented, "I'm afraid my partner will ridicule me if I tell him how I really feel or will regard what I admit to be my deep feelings as shallow, childish, or foolish—or even not true. Many times he has said, 'You can't feel that way. That's the stupidest thing I've ever heard!' Statements like this prevent my being totally honest. I fear rejection more than lack of understanding, so I usually say what I think he wants me to say."

When we cover up our real feelings or pretend that things are better than they are, we are playing dangerous emotional games. Learning to maintain our integrity requires considerable effort, which includes listening to our anger.

Case Study

Gary and Lynda Miller are both Introverted-Feeling people who experience many silent angers but resist or ignore their friendly warnings. Lynda expects Gary to behave and speak the way she thinks and acts, implying that hers is the proper, mature, or best way. She innocently assumes a parental role, which makes him feel inferior and childish. Lynda's scoldings or put-downs not only embarrass Gary and hurt his feelings but also create resentment toward her.

Gary is reluctant to admit his hurt to Lynda for fear she will belittle him all over again or re-scold him, which would indicate that she doesn't care if he is uncomfortable—a subconscious fear of most Feeling people.

When Gary does bring up an offense, Lynda reacts by countering with a strong defense of her position. "You shouldn't get hurt feelings when I try to help you," she defends. Parental "you" statements directed to adult mates stir up anger and invite additional resentments. (Later in this book I'll discuss parent and child roles in adult relationships).

Lynda resents hearing that she is responsible for hurting Gary. That creates guilt—a common anger warning. Gary is afraid her second put-down will be even worse than the first, so he bottles his hurt and clams up, preferring peace at any cost. Since Lynda responds negatively to Gary's defensive retreat with her own version of unapproachable silence, their communication reaches a stalemate. They are fighting the signals, and neither will break the silence.

Two such introverts need to decide ahead of time that the offended one will automatically become the spokesperson. Waiting until the one who has offended realizes that the other person is hurting stymies communication.

"I love Gary too much to risk belittling him again," Lynda said. "I'll just not say anything critical. I'd rather dislike how he's acting or speaking than feel guilty about hurting his feelings. I'll just learn to tolerate what goes on. That's easier."

Yes, how unfortunate it would be if Lynda completely ignored Gary's actions or words that distress and embarrass her. Gary benefits greatly from Lynda's opinions, encouragements, cautions, and approval. But he needs to be assured that Lynda's comments are meant to help rather than ridicule. It is her timing and wording that need refinement.

Utilizing Magic "I" Statements

With practice, Lynda can avoid taking offense when Gary reveals that her comments hurt his feelings. Rather than defend herself after Gary reacts negatively to her rebukes, Lynda can acknowledge his angry but honest feelings regarding her offensive parental attitude by using "I" statements such as:

- "I would never want to hurt you."
- "I'm sorry you felt put down."
- "I regret that I was insensitive to your feelings."

Whether or not Lynda feels guilty—and whether or not she is guilty—this non-offensive attitude will encourage Gary to be totally honest, instead of bottling up his angry frustrations. A non-accusatory gentleness will make it possible for Lynda to get in touch with Gary's deepest feelings.

Confrontational episodes can be eliminated completely if Lynda masters the non-offensive, adult method of expressing her angry feelings of disappointment in Gary's behavior by avoiding accusatory "you" statements and using nonthreatening magic "I" statements instead:

- "I don't agree with you."
- "I was embarrassed by your story."
- "I don't appreciate your negativism."
- "I feel uncomfortable when you act hurt and abused."

As Gary and Lynda practice substituting adult responses, their relationship will quickly blossom. To maintain open communication, the Millers must trust each other enough to share their feelings and then consider the other's suggestions. (We will discuss tenderhearted men in greater detail in the next chapter).

Theodore Rubin says that expressing one's anger reveals respect for the individual in question and strengthens confidence. So, calmly and kindly expressing one's anger increases confidence that the relationship is important and strong enough to withstand future conflicts and bumps in the road. Increased understanding is the catapult toward getting along with everyone.

Releasing Stored Anger

Anger is a sign that we are alive and well; hate is a sign that we are sick and need to be healed, so advises Lewis B. Smedes in *Forgive and Forget*.

We do ourselves a favor to learn how to forgive and forget, actually forgive and not mention. A grudge represents the unresolved or unexpressed anger we feel toward someone we believe has wronged us. It is the emotional scab we fuss at until it becomes infected, damaging our relationships and possibly our health.

Getting rid of a grudge resembles the operation of spraying for plant diseases. Definite action has to be taken. But how? Before losing our cool or retreating into silent anger, we should consider the following checklist:.

- Acknowledge the problem: Are you sure it was intentional?
- Consider the source: Do you respect the other person(s)?
- Look at the situation from the other person's perspective: Is he or she uninformed?
- Determine the seriousness of the deed, word, or slight.
- Write down the pros and cons of your proposed solution.
- Weigh the benefits of the solution against the risks:
  Will this help you or the other person?

- Confront the person. Write a letter if dealing with an iNtuitive. Be brief if dealing with a Thinker. Use a soft approach if dealing with a Feeler. Use facts and number them when dealing with a Sensing person. Give an introvert plenty of time to reply. Be prepared for an extrovert's prompt verbal response.
- Endeavor to become an expert in using non-offensive magic "I" statements until they flow with ease.

Since the person one has a grudge against is sometimes unaware of the offense, or if aware isn't bothered enough to try to fix the problem, it falls to the offended person to propose a way to make up for the perceived injury. This would involve presenting a compromise, which means bringing up the offense or discussing a solution. Just acknowledging someone's bitter statement eases a situation and permits either agreement or agreement to disagree.

Anger and Forgiveness

We are never so free as when, of our own volition, we reach back into our past and forgive a person who has caused us pain and engendered our resentment. Cherished resentments mature into diseased grudges that stifle growth and relationships, as Robyn's story illustrates:

"My parents always took us to church. We were never allowed to miss anything. It was really boring much of the time, too. But after we children all left home, I noticed that my parents stopped going to church except for Sunday mornings.

"When I asked my dad about this inconsistency, he said, 'We had to be a good example to you then.' This confuses me, and it doesn't seem fair that they made us go and just pretended to like what they were making us do."

After acknowledging that her parents had done their best, just as she was attempting to do with her own children, Robyn was able to forgive her parents for their hypocrisy.

The only way to heal the pain that will not heal itself is to forgive the person who hurt you. Forgiving stops the reruns of pain. Like Naomi in the previous chapter who released her mother from childhood resentments by using the empty-chair method, even a 20-year-old weight can be lifted from your emotional shoulders.

Forgiving heals your memory because it changes your memory's vision. When you release the wrongdoer from the wrong, you cut a malignant tumor out of your inner life. You set a prisoner free. When you do, you will discover that the real prisoner was yourself.

A minister friend of mine describes forgiveness as the garbage disposal built into one's spiritual life. We flush out the resentments by forgiving. When you no longer need to talk about someone's offense, this is a sign that forgiveness has taken place. A twinge of anger as you recall the circumstances becomes a warning that can both prevent the wrong from happening to you again and initiate some long-overdue forgiveness on your part.

Regarding forgetting, many people never actually forget past offenses, but over time they realize they have no unction to mention the offense or name the offender. You'll be pleased to know that those painful memories, along with hurt, will also fade away over time.

Peacemaking Anger

Admitted and controlled anger is a positive way toward achieving better relationships. It can teach, release, refine, and encourage us toward peacemaking action. Appreciating and using our angry feelings in a positive way can stimulate us to reach out to help a mistreated person (even if it's our own self), but can also render constructive assistance to the offender.

Spiritual maturity includes choosing what we will allow to visibly upset us, then controlling how we express our feelings to guarantee the greatest benefit to all concerned. Learning to exercise emotional control enables us to gently and honestly express our feelings of anger before allowing resentments to take root.

We would do well to decide at the beginning of each day that we will allow feelings of anger to catch our attention and teach us something more about ourselves. Managing anger constructively and with optimism leads to peacemaking. "But the wisdom that comes from heaven is first of all pure; then peace-loving, considerate, submissive, full of mercy and good fruit, impartial and sincere. Peacemakers who sow in peace raise a harvest of righteousness" (Jas. 3:17-18).

Properly managed anger purges and cleans out our emotional beings. Listen to what Christine learned from slowly, promptly, and positively respecting her anger warnings, thereby resisting resentment and rejection:

"Familiar taunts of 'Moby Dick' and 'Whale' greeted me as I made my way across the parking lot. Usually, I rail out against such mocking in a rage and blind fury. Today, however, I calmly walked over to the crowd of teenagers and said, 'Okay, I know I'm overweight. But how would you like it if you were all by yourself and a group of persons made fun of you? If the tables were turned, I wouldn't do that to you.'

"The feeling of self-esteem at having stood up for myself was really good. Expressing that anger without verbal abuse toward them or letting it remain inside and fester was a real relief. One of the teenagers stepped out and said he was sorry and that he thought the whole group should be ashamed. I felt really purged by allowing my anger to be released in a healthy, honest way. The group was helped, and so was I."

After reading my discussion on constructive anger, a 30-year-old INFJ client emailed the following comments:

"Wow, I had no idea how much I have to do with anger. I didn't realize fully until now how much anger has affected my life, my being. It has almost destroyed my life at times over the years. The chapter is very helpful at clarifying common misconceptions of which I was a deep holder as a Feeler.

"As a child I was deeply angry about my parents' ideas and their anger at each other and how they handled it. As a tenderhearted girl, though, I didn't want to risk losing any more love or living through any more conflict. I saw how miserable anger was, so I tried to deny and stifle my own inside me for many years.

"I felt ashamed to be angry. Anger was wrong. I tried to be sweet and would constantly say, 'It's okay, don't worry about it' or I would make excuses to my parents or take the blame myself.

"I see now, though, that anger does not necessarily mean that you don't love the person—or vice versa if they are angry at you. In fact, it can be quite the opposite. It's ok. It's not the end of love, the relationship, or life. What a relief! There's nothing to hide.

"I especially appreciated how you pointed out anger's side effects of virtually bringing your life to a complete stop; that's what it has done to mine. I have had so many relationship problems and problems of getting through my own day—problems of guilt—all because of anger and guilt associated with it. So many paths and knee-jerk reactions have been subconsciously developed inside me over these years, like how I react when I'm offended. The easiest, or at least best way, is to handle it immediately and not hold it inside. Then maybe it could only be a passing shower instead of a hurricane."

In our garden of relationships, the end result is worth every ounce of effort. The next chapter is particularly dedicated to the minority tenderhearted men and logic-minded women who suffer substantially from people who either reject or try to change them.

CHAPTER 8

Tenderhearted Men and Logic-Minded Women: Selective Pruning

If it is possible, as far as it depends on you,
live at peace with everyone.
Romans 12:18

"Describe your mother in one word or phrase," a preacher urged in a Mother's Day message. Jan's 11-year-old son sitting next to her responded with a spontaneous half-giggle.

"Did you think of something?" Jan whispered expectantly, pleased to know he had been listening.

"Yeah," he nodded quickly without looking up.

"I'd be interested in your description of me, Tim," his mother probed eagerly as she drove the family home. Tim was the youngest of four, the child to whom she felt she had given the most adequate attention. She could use a good compliment, too, considering that no one except the minister had yet mentioned Mother's Day.

"That's alright," he said with a disinterested shrug.

"No, I really want to know what you thought," Jan encouraged, knowing that 11-year-olds resist sharing in front of their siblings. "No one will laugh at you," she assured. "Honestly, Tim, it would really help me to know how you perceive me."

"Okay," he agreed reluctantly under her pressure. "Nag."

"That's it?" Jan responded in disbelief. She was so shocked that she impulsively let up on the gas pedal. No one else said anything.

"I can't believe what I just heard," she resisted.

"It's true!" Tim reiterated with renewed confidence. "You're always on my case."

A big lump squeezed into Jan's throat. She was silent the rest of the way home, startled not only by his reply but also disappointed and hurt. How could he say such a thing after all she had done for him?

Women resent the nag tag or domineering label by anyone.

Are You a Nag?

An informal survey among a small group reveals different perceptions of the meaning of nagging:

- "Nagging is telling me to do what I plan to do anyway," one gentleman said. "In about two years," he added with a grin.
- "Nagging is complaining about my grades and bugging me to do unimportant things," a teenager offered.
- "Nagging is disagreeing with me," a third person commented.
- "Nagging is reminding people of things they would regret if they forgot," an insightful mother explained in her own defense.
- "Nagging is when you won't let me forget what I want to forget," her mate countered, then added, "Nagging is you, you, you; do, do, do."
- "Nagging is the perception by a person who deems a repetitive request as frivolous or inconsequential," a pompous executive defined unhesitatingly.
- "Nagging is helping my family members stay on schedule and get things finished so they are not embarrassed and others are not inconvenienced with extra responsibilities," a mother of teens defended.
- "Nagging is trying to get me to do something I'd prefer not to do—like dressing up or going someplace I don't enjoy—or trying to get me to stop something I do enjoy—like picking my teeth, spitting, belching, or wiping my mouth with my sleeve," an elderly man summarized.
- "Nagging is just trying to get people to do what's best for them, like getting enough sleep, eating the right kind of food, getting the proper exercise, wearing a jacket in pneumonia weather," a grandmother suggested.

With such varied opinions, let's check a dictionary definition of nag: "To pester or annoy by constant scolding, complaining, or urging. To torment with anxiety, discomfort, or doubt. To scold, complain, or find fault constantly. To be a continuing source of discomfort, anxiety, or annoyance. A person, especially a woman, who nags." Can you believe that? My source happens to be *The American Heritage Dictionary* (a late-1960s edition, obviously). Some common naggings ascribed to females are:

- "You need to fasten your seat belt."
- "You should exercise."
- "You ought to call/write your mother."
- "Clean your room before you leave."

- "When are you going to cut the grass?"
- "You must take your bath."
- "Slow down."
- "Turn that music down."
- "Get off that cell phone."

If you'll notice, most of these nagging statements begin with the word "you" or the understood "you" and use war words such as should, ought, must, and need. That is why they are so offensive. So, anyone wanting to eliminate nagging from their character analysis, and thereby see action, can accomplish both by substituting I prefer/wish/want/think/feel statements. We are all guilty of nagging someone about something sometime—like broken records:

- Children nag mothers about "How long till we eat?"
- Mothers nag children about cleaning up their room.
- Fathers nag family members about turning off the lights.
- Bosses nag secretaries to finish reports.
- Secretaries nag bosses about returning calls.
- Wives nag husbands about fixing things or carrying out the trash.
- Husbands nag wives to hurry up or stop wasting money.
- Parents nag grown-up children about getting married.
- Parents nag married children to present grandchildren.
- Grandparents nag young people to slow their pace.
- Teachers nag students to finish their projects and homework.

Why is it that it is usually a woman who is tagged (sometimes unfairly) with a nag label? "I'd rather be accused of caring too much or being overly protective than to be called a nag," many women confide. In fact, some women counter that men are also whiny, complaining, or picky. Yes, without a doubt, certain men easily fit the nagging role. However, worry-wart men are called concerned or sensitive. Women with the same tendencies are nags.

Heart-Logic males and females alike, more than Thinking people, have a great tendency to nag as well as to acquiesce to another's nagging. Consequently, some men are actually more comfortable and feel safer with a woman who takes charge and keeps them reminded of their responsibilities.

Many naggers are like Jan—completely unaware of it. Their sense of responsibility, desire for approval, or fear of displeasing someone presses them into the nagging mold by people who depend on them.

Domineering Males and Females

In addition to nagging, many women resent being labeled as domineering. Are these two offenses the same? Consider this definition from my pre-feminist dictionary: "Domineer: To rule over arbitrarily or arrogantly; tyrannize. To dominate, control, implying superior authority or power. To be lord and master."

Interestingly enough, this definition implies that domineering is a male attribute. Nagging and domineering are closely related, though not synonymous. Comparing these two definitions carefully, we discover that to domineer actually reflects authoritarian attitudes, for example:

• "Don't ask questions; just do what I say."
• "My way is the only way."
• "I can blow up if I want to, because I'm in charge."
• "You're the weak one; I've got all the facts and the money."
• "Shut up and listen to how it's going to be!"

All these statements carry a message: "I am stronger and smarter than you, so you have no choice but to submit to my power." Domineering tactics are just as unpopular as nagging and likewise exhibit little concern toward the person being manipulated.

Keep in mind that domineering and nagging are twin affronts to females. Women counterattack by denouncing some males for their fierce tempers, closed minds, and evident disregard for feelings—a stereotypical modern-male macho personality.

Of course, many women resent male counterparts who arrogantly discredit their opinions or abilities and overlook their feelings. However, men are rarely described as domineering, but rather as decisive and serious executives and bosses or strong leaders in their homes or work world. Men who control by domineering are praised for being in charge, whereas directive women are tagged negatively.

Many tenderhearted people, without acknowledgment, are more secure with stern, austere Thinkers to back them up. Yet, at the same time, they chafe under any immature Thinker's self-centered, cold logic.

Feeling people regard domineering as a serious fault, but Thinkers are convinced that nagging is much worse. Nevertheless, I have never heard anyone project that his or her goal in life is to develop either characteristic, although some people manage to be both! Our aim should be to understand and adjust to others, not control them.

Of the many so-called domineering women I have interviewed—many of whom admit that the accusation of nagging or domineering is true—most consider themselves to be domineering by choice. Most domineering behavior is rooted in a perceived need to nag those who procrastinate or are lazy or undisciplined.

Actually, all temperaments—male and female—have the potential to be either way, given the right situation. Disregard or misunderstanding of the power struggles between various preferences—Extroverted / Introverted, Sensing / iNtuitive, Head-Logic / Feeling Heart-Logic, Structured / sPontaneous—is a subtle and neglected issue involving healthy communication.

Just as superfluous and invasive foliage in a garden must be periodically trimmed to allow for the healthy development of individual plants, in the interest of harmonious living, certain human traits must be controlled by selective pruning. So it is with domination and nagging; they both rob relationships of rapport, growth, and beauty by blocking creative communication.

Many men (and women) are clamoring to be released, freed to be who they really are. However, we have to find a way to eliminate these negative annoyances without destroying or upsetting the healthy balance of respect, direction, and valuable assistance.

Unfortunately, irritating excesses will not merely fall away. They must be gently trimmed with understanding and replaced with positive adult responses girded by a loving and patient attitude.

As already established, producing a lovely display of domestic flower gardens depends on such expert human attention as watering, weeding, and spraying. Another critical behind-the-scenes step in maintaining beautiful growth is that of pruning. Unless plants are skillfully, tenderly, and regularly shaped—especially when they are young—they will appear shabby in appearance, even though they may be very healthy.

Pruning a plant closely parallels what needs to be done with the habits of nagging and domineering. Just a little introspection will reveal that all of us could probably use a bit of pruning in those areas. Or, perhaps learning how we can diplomatically resist another's nagging and domineering ways and also encourage his or her self-pruning might be what we want to learn.

Issues and Answers

Since women seem to bear the greater burden of being labeled nagging and domineering, let's investigate the conditions that can provoke these behaviors. We will concentrate on the primary seedbed—home—and gain insight through several case studies into both the causative elements and possible solutions to the problem.

The Nagging Memory Bank

Tearfully, Jan recounted her problem: "What a terrible Mother's Day I had yesterday," she moaned. "Tim completely ruined it. Could it be true that I'm a nag?" she questioned. "I've tried to be a good mother, but evidently I'm failing miserably. Tim would forget his head if it were not attached. Is it wrong for me to help him remember things?"

"Why not thank Tim for being honest?" I suggested. "Admit that you didn't realize you had become a nag—always on his case. Tell him you really appreciate his drawing your attention to the problem. You might say, 'If there's anything I don't want to be, it's a nag.'

"Then, promise him: 'With your cooperation and encouragement, Tim, I'm willing to do whatever it takes to whip this problem, because the last thing I want to do is boss you around. In order to succeed, though, I'll need your help and cooperation. I've put an alarm clock in your room so you can get yourself up, which will keep me from bugging you in the morning. I'll stop hurrying you to breakfast or telling you when to leave for school.'"

I also advised Jan to promise not to nag her son about putting his clothes in the laundry and to stop hanging up his clothes and straightening his room. In fact, she was to tell him she would stay out of his room entirely so that she would not be tempted to criticize.

I also suggested that Jan promise her son to try very hard not to ask about his homework and that she would stop making trips to school to deliver a forgotten gym bag, trumpet, books, or lunch.

"If I nag you about anything," Jan told Tim, "please let me know. "

Near the end of that historic week, and after three tardies and a couple of missed lunches, Tim said, "Mom, I really need your help. I just can't remember everything or get everything done. I guess nagging isn't so bad after all."

Because Tim had chosen to depend on his mother's memory and unconsciously expected her to think for him, he had pressed her into the nagging role. Not too surprisingly, he resented her doing the very things he relied on her to do.

In the future, though, Jan needs to let Tim take some lumps for forgetting things. And she should constantly be weaning him away from depending on her to make up for his own irresponsibility. She can avoid the nagging syndrome by making requests rather than commands: "I would like your room cleaned up," rather than "You need to clean up your room."

Jan is like many Structured mothers who just want the house kept neat and tidy and their children to learn to take care of routine responsibilities. When children fail or are sloppy, disrespectful to others, or lazy, the mother feels somehow responsible, so she beefs up the nags.

The principle to remember is: prune while plants are young. Trim your nagging and domineering tendencies before they become full grown by substituting "I prefer" statements for "You should, ought, must, or need" commands.

As you read the following examples of nagging and/or domineering, apply the principles outlined in Jan and Tim's experience—listening, respect, honesty, communication using non-offensive "I" statements—to see how these situations could have been modified or even completely avoided

The Self-Appointed Manager

Phil Martin was distraught because his wife wanted a divorce. The Martins had been married for 20 years, and their only child was away in college. He could not understand why Grace had left him, because (as far as he knew) everything had always gone well for them. Phil, an ISFP (Rose / Sympathizer)—independent with a friendly, fun-loving, and generous personality—was very attractive to Grace, an ISTJ (Aster / Conscientious Worker)—very private, serious, decisive, and dependable, and whose word was her bond.

Because Phil put off making difficult decisions or getting started on routine duties, Grace gradually assumed more and more responsibility for running the home. She took over the finances to avoid late charges accrued because of Phil's procrastination in bill paying. She detested wasting money. Although she worked full time outside the home, Grace also managed the housework, cooking, marketing, and laundry. She even assisted with the outside maintenance.

It bugged Grace that Phil needed reminders to get the car inspected, snow tires removed, grass cut, and so on. It galled her even more that he let household repairs slide. He preferred to make fun decisions about where they would go on vacation and vehicle and recreation purchases, especially those involving his truck.

Grace's resentment intensified as Phil always found time to watch TV, nap, play golf, and fish—even though there were jobs to complete—while she allowed herself no personal free time until work was done, which was never. Phil did not volunteer to do much around the house because he knew Grace liked the way she did things. But they never talked about these conflicts because they were both introverts. Phil also avoided arguments whenever possible.

Rather than nag, Grace silently seethed with anger over Phil's resistance to making difficult decisions and his failure to complete routine duties. She gradually became the typical, but silent, domineering mate. (ISTJs believe that everyone should carry his or her share of the load.) Her unspoken and unfulfilled expectations produced a huge crop of resentments.

Meanwhile, as Phil acquiesced to Grace's managerial abilities, he became more dependent on her, which made her feel responsible for everything involving his welfare.

"I dislike being totally in charge," Grace admitted. "I really wish that Phil would help make more decisions. I keep hoping that he will grow up, but he seems to get more dependent all the time."

The Martins could have avoided their deep-seated problems if they had understood their inborn lifestyle preferences. Grace's desire to finish work before play need not have threatened Phil.

Rather than taking over responsibilities that her husband shirked, had Grace been willing to allow and expect him to handle the finances the way sPontaneous people like Phil prefer (despite possible late charges) and to refuse to make every decision, he would have been forced to bear his share and would thereby feel better about himself.

Grace eventually decided that since she had a good job, was handling the chores, and making most of the decisions, she could manage without her husband. Yet Phil had no idea how unhappy and disappointed Grace had been. He figured everything was okay because she rarely complained. One good aspect of nagging is that at least the other person hears when everything is not alright.

If either of these two people had expressed their basic expectations—he for more affection and she for more assistance with decision making—they could have exposed and resolved many of their differences. (This is a typical problem of introverts.) However, a parent-child marriage just does not work.

The Substitute Parent

Eugene, an ENFP (Chrysanthemum / Catalyst), creates the climate that demands his wife's control over his "little boy" ways. "Don't forget to get me up for work," Eugene would remind Frances, an ENFJ (Poppy / Encourager). His mother always woke him for school or work.

Frances would call Eugene after she got to work, to make sure he got up in time to open his business. Accepting the responsibility for waking a husband or teen is the first step toward becoming a domineering woman.

Eugene refuses to hang up his clothing or put laundry in the hamper, make the bed (he's the last one out), or clean the tub, rationalizing that he doesn't want to be "bossed around." He defends: "It's not because I want to hurt Frances. I just don't want her to tell me what and when to do things. I regard that as nagging and domineering. I got enough of that direction when I was a kid."

As a tenderhearted mate, Eugene wants what he does to be noticed and appreciated. If he does something because Frances requested it, the behavior ceases to be his idea and something worthy of praise. "If I hear no mention of what I did, I assume she didn't notice, so I quit," Eugene added. "It's her work, anyway."

As an extrovert, Eugene often mentions what he does, but because Frances is angry that he rarely waits on himself or helps her with keeping the house going (as she thinks he should), she withholds praise. Heart-Logic men need regular praise, but Frances doesn't know this.

"Eugene will only fix something after I've yelled about it for several days—maybe weeks," Frances complained. "I usually don't praise him, because I have so much trouble getting him to do what he should do without being told. He's a grown man. I feel that I should be complimented on getting him to do it."

Frances has not only become a nagging mother, but also a domineering mate. Taking into consideration that many iNtuitive men find repairing and doing physical things difficult should help Frances ease up on her expectations.

"When Eugene is offended or feels unappreciated," Frances said, "he punishes me by hiding in his workroom. He doesn't like to take his licks. He hates to be blamed for any problem. Boy, do I feel like I have a child on my hands," she exclaimed. "This is more than I bargained for."

Some partners have the attitude that their mates are their responsibility to teach. However, since they have already been taught by their mother, grandmothers, and teachers, a mate's job is to adjust to what already exists … another parent-child relationship in disarray.

The Disappointed Enabler

"My partner shared a business with his brother to breed dogs, even though I was against it," Jana, an ISFJ (Tulip / Server), shared about Howard, an ESFP (Daisy / Performer). "I was against the idea because I know how irresponsible Howard is, but we really needed the income. I hated to invest the little bit of money we had saved, but he promised me that this time he wouldn't disappoint me.

"After a few days he fell into his old pattern of getting up late for work, so he'd ask me to feed the dogs," Jana said with a heavy sigh. "I didn't like to but I did it, mainly to encourage him and prove that I believed in him.

"Then he'd forget to pick up the dog food, so I'd do that, too, and later was forced into taking the dogs to the vet and on and on. It wasn't easy with a two-year-old and being five months pregnant. I didn't complain for a good while because I didn't want to be a nag like my mother and his mother were. But when I realized that Howard considered it my responsibility to take care of the dogs every day—not our agreement at all—I really let loose and complained and yelled at him every day, not that it did any good.

"The dogs were noisy and scrappy, and taking care of them was clearly Howard's project. He knows a lot about dogs; I know nothing. Yet he took all the credit for the good things I did and yelled at me when something wasn't done right.

"When his brother complained about the neglect of the dogs, Howard blamed me for every problem that developed. He kept reminding me that he was head of the house and that I was supposed to do what he said. Some head!" she added cynically. "Because we lost a couple of newborn puppies, we lost our part in the business. Naturally, it was all my fault.

"I just hate to be Howard's slave. He expects me to fill the gaps of whatever he leaves undone, which does not just involve the dogs. He doesn't pick up his clothes or put his tools away. I have to follow behind him. If I remind him of things, I shouldn't; if I fail to remind him, I should have. I can't win," Jana shrugged.

Wives are wise to remind their partners, "I love you too much to allow you to shirk your responsibilities." Again, honest communication and a refusal to do what is agreed the other will do (except in emergencies) force the dependent mate into adulthood. Howard and Jana have a relationship that is primarily child to child; marriage is for adults.

The Female Chairperson

"I expect you to make the household financial decisions," Frank, an INFP (Portulaca / Idealist) informed Rita, an ENFJ (Poppy / Encourager), after they returned from their honeymoon.

"What does Frank do after my first month's check but buy a brand-new truck? On credit, of course. He also bought a big compressor. I found a second job, not because I wanted to get out of doing housework, but because we needed help paying bills. I'm so frustrated with Frank's lack of financial savvy.

"He's aware of my struggle with balancing the finances but still wants the freedom to buy fun things. I do not like to be in charge of finances, but if I am, I want a little cooperation from him.

"This arrangement did not make sense to me at the time, until I took a hard look at how Frank's mother and father functioned. Then it became clear why Frank thought this was normal.

"His mother was the financial head of their home. When she wanted new furniture, she picked it out and had it delivered. When she wanted an appliance, she did the same thing. She carried the money, the credit cards, paid all the bills, and made the phone calls. When the children needed money for anything, they went to her. Frank's father was happy for his wife to make those decisions; it made life simpler for him.

"Frank complains that I nag him to death and look at life too seriously. What can we do to change this situation?"

Nagging easily develops when two people embrace different value systems. Feeling persons put up with things that don't make sense because they believe in peace at any cost. But Rita couldn't avoid nagging when the finances were unnecessarily in disarray.

Through counseling, this couple discovered that not only their differences in personality makeup but also discussing Frank's family financial systems uncovered the root problem. The couple agreed to talk with a financial planner and set up a budget where they shared equal roles of responsibility. Thus, arguments and Rita's need for nagging ended.

The bottom line is: what worked for some parents may not work for their offspring. Again, marriage does not work well when one partner is a parent and the other a child.

The Neglected Mate

"What bothers me about Larry," Loretta, an ISFP (Rose / Sympathizer), said, "is that he never looks at me. That drives me up the wall. It makes me feel like I'm not a person who counts. And he's not a firm-enough disciplinarian with the children. I get tired of doing it all the time, and because I have to, I start yelling and I can get pretty nasty. I feel like an ogre. I try to communicate my feelings and wants, but he just doesn't pick up on them. I think Larry wants me to feel good about myself, but he says really hurtful things to me and even hits me. I feel he has a lot of hurt, anger, and resentment from his childhood—more than he wants to admit—and he takes those feelings out on me.

"I do talk to him like I'm his mother because he forgets everything or does not get the instructions straight when I ask him to do something before I come home from work. When I'm in a hurry, I bark commands but don't mean anything by it. He takes it too personally.

"He hates my yelling. He slams doors, punches walls, and breaks things in the house. I've done this recently also, but only because I get so frustrated with him. I can't take much more. If he'd only let me know that I am special, take me out sometimes, or buy me a present. But I guess he doesn't think I deserve it," she heaved a big sigh through her tears.

Larry, an ISTP (Gladiola / Unstoppable Operator), was not a fan of counseling until the facts and future were irrefutable. Any time a mate strikes another, outside help is a given. Larry understood it was better to submit to counseling rather than have Loretta report domestic violence and possibly receive a protective order.

Larry and Loretta, opposite in only one preference, have lots of communication but it's all negative. She tells him how she feels, but only in a nagging way, which he rejects. They take turns acting like each other's parent, then like children. Marriage is not for parents or children.

The solution to their problem was simple: Understand who the other is and pledge to keep the dialogue kind with the use of "I" statements. Loretta needs to be open and honest about what she would like to hear from Larry, where she would like to go with him, and her desire for gifts. Sensing Thinkers want their mates to be happy, but they need help to know what it requires.

Domineering Women

In my experience, a tenderhearted male tends to draw out the protective nature of a female. Therefore, a mother often goes to bat for a sensitive son and protects him from taking his lumps from his father, siblings, and friends.

If men—while boys—get used to having female protection, affection, and personal attention, they expect it from their mates. Many wives, "motherly" by nature, are delighted to continue giving TLC and are attracted to men who want the attention they dispense. Helping someone who appreciates and needs support gives a Feeling person a sense of self-worth. But after a while, the wife may feel uneasy when her husband allows others, including herself, to take advantage of him. The wife of a tenderhearted man may fault him for not standing up for himself but in the same breath criticize him for getting into arguments about her own tendency to dominate him.

"I really wish Norman would tell me 'no' sometimes," Kay sighed. "I know I'm not always right, but he just goes along with whatever I decide since it's understood that he doesn't intend to make the decisions. He says that he prefers to do it my way rather than have any hassle. I am forced to make decisions whether I want to or not. I've learned how, but I still don't like it. I'd like to lean on him once in a while. I hate to be the final boss, but someone has to run things, and he won't."

In such a situation, children generally adopt the mother's attitude and are likely to lose respect for their dad when he doesn't project his opinions and insist on bearing some of the weight of household decision making. However, they may also resent the mother for assuming leadership and unconsciously blame her for their father's passive ways.

"When the children ask you if they can go someplace or do something, what do you usually say?" is a question I've asked many men who have accused their mate of being domineering. Invariably they reply, "I tell them to ask their mother."

"So, who has put her in charge?" I challenge.

"I get your point," Norman admitted.

Mothers who get used to being in charge resent the fact that the father-figure in the home has reneged on his share of the responsibility—a parental drop-out. The more insecure the wife feels about this, the more inadequate the husband feels, especially if she complains. The more inadequate he feels, the more domineering the woman becomes. Thus the cycle continues, and this is the heart of many marital break-ups. Often, womanizing and/or alcoholism or drug abuse are by-products of a man's feelings of inadequacy and fears about his "masculinity."

For her own good, as well as her partner's, the mate of a compliant man must avoid making his decisions. She should share her thoughts and ideas with him but refrain from assuming responsibility for his agreed-upon areas of responsibility.

Statements such as "I prefer not to decide," "I feel more comfortable if you handle this," or "I have confidence in your judgment" will tactfully encourage a laid-back mate to use logical decision making. (My book, *Encouragement: A Wife's Special Gift*, discusses this critical dimension at length.)

Sometimes it is "good ole Mom" who bears the weight of the entire household's complaints: "When are you going to shop, Mom? We've been out of cereal for weeks. I'm tired of peanut butter sandwiches, too. Can't we get some lunch meat?" or "Mom, can I please go? Everyone's going, and I need to know right away."

Older teens might nag sPontaneous-iNtuitive mothers: "Mom, this house looks like a pig sty. I'll never bring my friends here until it's decent." Or, as older teen Wayne groaned, "Isn't there anything in this house to eat? What kind of a mother are you?"

Husbands regularly nag their wives, rationalizing that "it's for their own good." The complaints are often about finances: "Honey, the bills are past due. We're going to have to pay late charges. You asked to do the books, remember?"

Many overweight mates have shared that their partner constantly puts them down and ridicules them for excess weight they have gained over the years. They are reminded over and over that something is full of calories—as though they have forgotten.

"I'd just like to see what would happen to their bodies after they gave birth to three or four kids," one irate wife declared.

"If he'd just give me a little sympathy and support instead of criticism and a sermon," another said, "I would be able to trim down faster. The more he reminds me that something is fattening, the more I want to eat it," she confessed.

Just as with men, women with alcohol or drug problems will often elicit domineering behavior from their friends and family, even little children. Though such nagging may be well-intended, it is usually ineffective.

The solution for all parties in a power struggle lies in open communication, which requires effort and cooperation on everyone's part.

Respect and communication are closely linked. Respect garners respect. In addition, if Feeling people will willingly cut away their annoying nagging (and some of the behavior that incites others to nag them), and if Thinking people will agree to lop off their intimidating authoritarianism, our garden of relationships, minus all kinds of domineering attitudes, will be free to produce a full harvest.

Though pruning can be painful, we can learn valuable lessons from the care given a flower garden. When we know how we nag, domineer, and annoy others, we will wisely cut away these irritations so that the richest communication and harmony can be realized.

Instead of wanting to rule the world, as some people fear, most "in charge" women just want cooperation, assistance, and appreciation in taking care of dual responsibilities.

Tenderhearted vs. Authoritarian Men

A large minority of men, 40 percent, by God's design prefer the Feeling preference. The world is a better place because of them, but special problems with relationships accompany their gifting.

Although nagging and complaining seem to come naturally to certain Feeling people, the problem seems to be intensified when two Feeling people co-exist. This may signify that two insecure people are trying to lean on each other.

"My wife was looking for someone to lean on, but she had to prop me up in order to lean on me," a Feeling man who understands temperament said. "I discovered," he added, "that if my wife knows I'm aware of what she expects, she will likely quit nagging."

When men understand what it is about them that causes women to become mother-hen-like and domineering, the art of pruning can begin on both sides.

Some Feeling men are intimidated by Thinkers of the same gender, so they resort to picking on the so-called weaker sex. Often, they talk tough and macho toward women so as to validate their ability to overpower someone. When a Thinking woman and a Feeling man marry, the insecurity dimension is usually lessened, because a female Thinker feels fairly secure, even without approval. Also, when a Feeling man understands the normalcy of male tenderheartedness, he may not wrestle as much with feelings of inadequacy.

Tenderhearted men have special problems if they believe they must prove their masculinity; the world is a warmer and more sensitive place because of them. It is quite clear, though, that domineering women are often a product of the dependency of Feeling men.

In all fairness to women, we must acknowledge that many men do nag and try to control women, wives, teens, children, and other men. Male bosses intimidate secretaries, male doctors intimidate nurses, and foremen intimidate those workers they supervise. There are fathers who browbeat and mentally abuse their children and partners, but many have no idea that they are the least guilty of doing so.

Logical Thinkers are capable of nagging with an authoritarian air. Women usually call it griping, growling, or hitting the ceiling. The offenders usually rationalize by saying they just want things right. Remember, Thinkers function well without harmony or others' approval.

A Thinker said to his mate, "You should know that nagging begets nagging," which was just his way to rationalize his authoritarian ways.

Head-Logic people often nag and criticize when a softhearted person persists in beating around the bush in making decisions or giving explanations.

Understanding Head-Logic Thinkers

Keep in mind that Thinkers are primarily designed with introverted emotions. They are confident in their abilities and are not concerned with pleasing people.

They may say, "If a decision pleases me, I'm satisfied. Even if others disapprove, that's the way it is. Give me enough facts to show me that my decision is inferior, and I'll change it. But just being agreeable isn't my style."

Thinkers prefer to make situation-based decisions rather than people-based decisions. The Head-Logic segment think about the thing they're going to do and not about others who are involved. Considering the people on the sidelines involves a little extra effort that Thinkers are willing to give only if they are reminded. In fact, thinkers are suspicious of those who use emotional argument to pressure them. They do not like to be manipulated or told what to do.

Sometimes Thinkers are unfairly accused of making cold decisions out of spite or to show who is in charge. They are just good at making impersonal cause-and-effect decisions. Our world would be in dire straits were it not for people who are capable of making hard-nosed, situation-based decisions.

Thinkers tend to be impatient with people who base their decisions merely on maintaining harmony or what would please another. As one executive observed, "I don't enjoy saying no, but I just trust my own judgment. Some decisions are not pleasant, but I know I need to improve on gift-wrapping my statements."

Male Thinkers

There are several key principles that can help in understanding male Head-Logic Thinkers:

• Structured-Thinking mates need to remember that sPontaneous-iNtuitives generally dislike routine housework and deadlines. STJs also have a tendency to take their families for granted, which is a fertile source for complaints.

• An ENTJ dad who nagged his ENFP daughter about a dusty piano or rumpled rugs would not allow her to put packages on the couch but insisted she take them directly to her bedroom before she hung up her coat. Nor was she allowed to kick her shoes off in the living room. ENTJs think they are pushing people in the right direction, but often they are pushing people around instead.

• An ISTJ dad who complained and growled to his ESFJ wife that she lets the kids sass her and allows them to be too noisy did not realize that an ESFJ parent thrives on any conversation and can tolerate a high noise level.

• INTJs, because of their introverted and iNtuitive bent for analytical perfection reinforced by Logical Structure, are not only difficult to please but also intimidate all other personalities except another NT. Mates, co-workers, and children gain their respect by not backing down, crying, or running away. Learning that INTJs express appreciation more by action than by words is the key to appreciating and understanding them.

• Pleasing an INTP with relaxed but strong Head-Logic can keep a worker, mate, friend, or child feeling inferior: "He tears down my work constantly, no matter what I do. My self-worth has sagged considerably." Family members or work associates do not have to apologize for their innate personality, but when they refuse to be backed down, the INTP will return respect.

Female Thinkers

Society tends to apply the label of "weak, weepy, and wrong" to females, but 40 percent of women do not fall into this category. So, when young girls wonder why they prefer to associate with guys rather than girls, it's often because the girls' Head-Logic preference seeks the common denominator.

When females say they rarely cry or feel strongly emotionally about sad situations, they are often criticized by other women. Being stern is very normal for Logic-Minded females whether they are Sensing or iNtuitive, Structured or sPontaneous, Extroverted or Introverted.

Logic-minded females deserve a special acknowledgment of their own struggles to understand how they differ from other females and how they yearn to be understood and respected by others. For instance, since INT females make up less than one percent of the general population, they struggle to fit in with Heart-Logic females and males alike.

After an INT business woman learned about her special gifting, she shared: "Understanding the idiosyncrasies common to INT females has helped me keep a sense of humor about myself and the puzzled look people sometimes have about my behaviors, abilities, or attitudes."

Logic-minded females, like Logic-minded males, rarely ask others for their opinions before making a decision. They defend, "I've thought it over and my answer is right." "The rest of the world isn't paying my bills, so I don't care how anyone feels about my decisions," a Thinking female business owner explained.

I wish for Logic-minded females to understand that they are wonderfully gifted for decision making, and we recognize that shouldering this responsibility is not easy. (You'll find more details on Logical Thinkers in my book, *Self-Esteem: Gift from God*.)

I encourage you to inform others that you do care about how people feel and that you appreciate where they're coming from; that your way of giving approval and making decisions, although legitimate, is not always understood or appreciated.

When Head-Logic persons are accepted and exposed to a steady diet of warmhearted and considerate decisions where people express their disappointments and feelings kindly, they more easily learn to consult the emotional-deciding process they possess as a lesser preference.

Thinkers reared in strong, emotional homes become quite proficient in using their sensitive side. All in all, Head-Logic deciders can display caring and consideration. They resemble rocks or bricks that must be warmed up periodically.

As we seek to understand Head-Logic Thinkers, the attempts to unify the 16 personalities as we live, love, and work together take on new meaning. Appreciating others resembles how we enjoy and adjust to radical changes in the weather.

Marriage Is for Adults

As promised, I'm closing this chapter with insights on how Thinking or Feeling decision-making preferences affect home relationships

As the examples reveal, some relationships struggle with one mate becoming the parent and the other behaving as a child. Sometimes the Feeling mate is afraid of his or her Thinking mate. Discussing this out-of-balance attitude puts the relationship on an adult-to-adult level.

Some relationships become parent to parent, with each mate wanting to boss the other. These couples don't fight; they just disagree. They don't get hurt; they just get mad. Each mate sticks to his or her decision, an ST to facts and an NT to reasons. An adult relationship would mean being kindly honest and learning the value of compromise. Compromising is not a weakness but adult-like.

In child-to-child partnerships, neither participant wants to be an adult. The partners take turns behaving helplessly or demanding. They often fight, cry, and then make up. Achieving an adult relationship demands that they agree to jointly apply Head-Logic practical decisions.

The only healthy relationship is that of adult to adult, when each partner is honest about how he or she feels, or thinks and expresses those opinions and feelings with non-offensive "I" statements. Communication is the most important ingredient for blending personalities and maintaining respect and self-esteem. Understanding and appreciating the innate differences of ourselves and others becomes the major goal for achieving healthy communication.

CHAPTER 9

Getting Along with Everyone: Adjusting to the Weather

My purpose is that they may be encouraged in heart and united in love,
so that they may have the full riches of complete understanding,
in order that they may know the mystery of God, namely, Christ,
in whom are hidden all the treasures of wisdom and knowledge.
Colossians 2:2-3

"One can take this temperament typing too seriously," Myrna declared. "Are we just to overlook someone's bad behavior, verbal slips, selfishness, arrogance, tardiness, slothfulness, stiffness, and all the other social blunders just because we know his or her type has a tendency toward it? Isn't it better, and simpler, for everyone to just try to live by the Golden Rule than to attempt to figure others out or excuse ourselves because of how we are?"

Truly, if everyone were honestly committed to living by the Golden Rule, there certainly would be a lot less tension. But hostilities, resentments, and misunderstandings exist, even among people who eagerly long for peace, harmony, and unity and try their best to achieve all three. All of us need tutoring in understanding and getting along with everyone.

Achieving a Climate of Respect and Self-Esteem

We can't drastically change anyone's behavior or attitudes, but we can avoid allowing others' preferences from overpowering ours and rendering us ineffective. By the same token, we can modify our behavior when we sense or learn that we overpower another's.

An excellent goal is to show due respect for others, ask for theirs in return, and work together toward mutual understanding and communication. Keep in mind that everyone, at times, experiences insecurities that present relationship challenges.

Just as plants in a flower garden must adjust to all sorts of weather and temperature changes, we humans need to learn all we can about our own personality and that of others and try to wield a positive influence by word, pen, and action.

I believe there is no such thing as incompatibility, but merely lack of understanding. Granted, blending some personalities is like backing two porcupines together—a close fit that demands fine tuning.

Only hermits can avoid interpersonal clashes and adjustment problems, which is probably their main reason for being hermits. Since everyone has been given a portion of all the personality preferences for physical and mental survival, blending of opposite tendencies is not as inconceivable as some people might believe.

Both plant and human life are dependent on water, light, and air. All three come in various forms and amounts and are not always pleasant or convenient to use. Sometimes those very elements are taxing or destructive.

To pursue our analogy, think of communication as water, information as light, and decision making as air. With a proper mixture, co-existence is possible and growth occurs. However, before these necessary elements can accomplish their task, the "soil" must be sweet and chemically balanced. Applying lime around the roots of a plant will sweeten a sour soil. With humans, proper understanding parallels the contribution of lime by reducing the acidity in a conflict-prone relationship. We will connect the flower motif as we discuss how to deal kindly with blending personalities.

Blending Preferences from Opposite Arenas: Extroversion and Introversion

In the discussion that follows, we will consider only the most difficult personality blends. If you read between the lines, you can apply the following sample combinations of blends to your own relationships involving marriage, parent-child, siblings, in-laws, co-workers, neighbors, and so on. Appreciate each other's unique abilities as well as limitations. Enjoy your discoveries. A client shared recently that she reads her profile repeatedly to learn who she is and that she reads her partner's profile to help her accept who he is.

Extroversion and Introversion: Structure in Common
ENFJ (Poppy / Encourager) and ISTJ (Aster / Conscientious Worker)

Blending Extroversion and Introversion demands compromise because extroverts need and can tolerate more people and noise than introverts. Extroverts are wise to fulfill their quota of people without obligating or faulting introverts. Introverts' frequent smileless silence is intimidating as well as puzzling, often causing extroverts to embrace incorrect assumptions. "Say something funny if you want me to smile," introverts often defend.

Being aware of these two opposite inborn preferences in families, the work world, and community activities will decrease tension and sweeten communication.

ISTJ introverts need more time to process what's been said and to formulate an appropriate response; ENFJ extroverts are wise to grant adequate time. Introverts should be reminded that extroverts are likely to say what they don't mean, and resist extracting hurt feelings from words too quickly spoken. ISTJs usually require a lot of time to think things over and may want to hand their opinions and ideas in written form to extroverts. ENFJs will probably organize their many thoughts and opinions on paper but speak them extemporaneously.

Extroversion and Introversion: Social Opposites
ESTJ (Geranium / Organizer) and INFP (Portulaca / Idealist)

"I never knew that turning on the radio as soon as we got in the car irritated Georgia so much," ESTJ Greg declared. "I would never have continued. Nor would I have talked on and on about nothing had I known I was violating Georgia's need for privacy. I also feel terrible to think back about how I exploded every time someone pulled out in front of me. My temper was close to the surface, and I ranted and raved so easily with no idea what I was doing to her. How she put up with me, I'll never know!" He sighed, as he looked in her direction.

"Believe me, it has been tough," INFP Georgia said quietly. "I just figured there was something wrong with me, because nearly everyone I know talks a lot. There were many times, though, when a headache saved me from accompanying Greg someplace. It was my way of avoiding an unpleasant situation. I guess I prefer headaches to burning anger and a feeling of inferiority," she laughed lightly. "That's probably why my headaches came in the first place," she analyzed. "My doctor often said they were caused by nerves."

"My only quiet time is after Greg goes to bed. He always criticizes me for staying up so late, especially because I can't get up with him in the morning. I realize now that sleeping late was another ploy to avoid his constant—not always pleasant— chatter. He is also less likely to turn on the radio or TV if I am still in bed."

"His talking is one reason I create excuses not to go places with him, too," Georgia confessed. "He not only talks nonstop at a party, but he's loud and tries to drag me into his conversation. I just don't like to talk, and drawing attention to me makes me feel all the more inferior," she continued.

"Now that I know Georgia doesn't like so much conversation, I can cut down on my endless comments," Greg volunteered.

"I would also like to be allowed to finish my sentences—another reason I say very little," Georgia interrupted.

"That's true," Greg admitted. "Since I assumed I was helping things move along, I never dreamed I was creating resentment. I am really sorry for being so crass and aggressive," he said sincerely. "I do hope you will forgive me, Georgia, and give me another opportunity to prove that I can be sensitive to your introversion."

After this dose of sweetening—and a climate change—Greg and Georgia's relationship will blossom in light of the information they have shared, automatically achieving adult-to-adult communication.

Two or Four Preferences in Common

When dealing with someone who shares the same four letters, you'll see eye to eye in most areas; however, too much togetherness will present boredom or stagnation of ideas. Knowing this will probably occur can signal that bringing people with opposite preferences into your friendships, work situations, or committee assignments will be a wise decision. For instance, a committee with all ESTJs will not make the wisest decisions involving feeling people.

Sensing-Thinking-Structured and iNtuitive-Feeling-Structured
ISTJ (Aster / Conscientious Worker) and INFJ (Camellia / Empathizer)

Carol needs approval from Calvin. She has given up a career to care for their preschool children. Keeping the house straight is not as easy as it once was and, even then, it never would satisfy an INFJ like Carol, who thrives on complex assignments.

Calvin works hard all day at being outgoing. When he comes home at night and is ready to crash, Carol is ready to cruise. Mentioning how hard she works and how lonesome she is upsets him because he cannot deliver what she wants: personal time with him.

They argue over the same things day after day. He insists that he is doing his share and just can't give any more. Then Carol wonders if her love for Calvin is slowly dying and she no longer feels important to him. Her self-esteem is at an all-time low because she has eliminated one big source: her career among adults. Though Calvin has not really changed from what he was while Carol worked outside the home, Carol notices his lack of verbal appreciation more since she's so bored and filled with self-pity.

"You mean after I've been politicking all day on my job, I have to push myself some more to give Carol a sense of importance? Having to do any more talking at home just grinds me the wrong way," Calvin muttered. "That's a big order!"

Verbal encouragement extended by Thinkers to Feelers transfers to wise investments that reap long-term dividends.

Introvert and Introvert
ISFP (Rose / Sympathizer) and ISFJ (Tulip / Server)

"We've had two weeks of silence," ISFP Sidney confessed. "So, you could say we've had no communication."

Obviously, a two-week silence is evidence of seriously disturbed communication, which always devastates a relationship. Silence is a childish technique, a form of anger to show that one is hurt.

"Sidney is not completely innocent," ISFJ Sonya said. "The reason I am silent is to avoid saying what I know I'll regret. After he demeans my family and insults me, I have nothing to say to him. That's why I go to bed early, alone."

"I never know what she's thinking because she doesn't ever tell me," Sidney explained. "Some nights I just stay in front of the TV, not knowing if she has gone to bed or if she will be coming to sit with me. On many nights I say to myself that she's mad at me so I might as well go play poker somewhere."

Introverted partners profit from incorporating a 10-minute "clear the air" time each evening before retiring. Honest sharing about the good and bad from the day is guaranteed to generate some discussion and release tensions that are certain to gather momentum—and turn sour—if left untouched. Since neither likes to go first, alternating is the first rule of the game. With each talking for an uninterrupted span of no longer than five minutes, the communication process will become easier with practice. This promotes an adult relationship.

If either has shared a grievance against the other, the listening mate may want to preface any defensive comments with "I hear you saying..." Repeating what she thinks she heard assures the injured party that he has been understood—and misinterpretation is less likely to occur. Some couples call this time their "dumping grounds," but the practice is wisely suggested in Ephesians 4: "Do not let the sun go down while you are still angry" (v. 26).

Two introverts like Sidney and Sonya tend to expect the worst to happen and may be pessimistic about many things. Being around other people may tire them, but Feeling decision makers need people to be brought into their lives to some extent—although the reasons for doing this will differ. ISFJs (like Sonya) want to serve and host, whereas ISFPs (like Sidney) prefer fun and physical action with other people but without much talk.

Sidney and Sonya need air, but making decisions based on cold, hard logic is their personality combination's hardest assignment—since neither prefers the Thinking preference. They will need to encourage each other to consult logic, but may experience a strong tugging at their heartstrings when making best decisions, even though they don't feel right.

The Lifestyle preference difference—the only one between Sidney and Sonya—will present a significant conflict about when to do things and finishing projects. The ISFJ will need to learn to be more flexible, whereas the ISFP will want to be more disciplined and time-conscious.

All of us have associations at home and work with people who are just a bit different, so accepting that they are as legitimate as we are provides a path to getting along with them.

iNtuitive and Structured
INTJ (Iris / Expert Strategist) and ENFJ (Poppy / Encourager)

ENFJ Celeste has enjoyed being at home with her children but is delighted to be back in the swing of the adult world of teaching where she can exchange ideas, which extroverted iNtuitives usually enjoy most. However, she feels guilty when the housework does not get finished and there is no time to play with the children as she used to.

She also feels guilty because she looks forward to going to work and really hates to go home and face all the homemaking duties. "When men work, they get promotions. When a mom stays home with house and kids, when does she ever get promotions?" Celeste asked. "I want to know that I'm important."

iNtuitives must always be making improvements, and recognition and reputation are very important to them. For Celeste, the main stimulation for cleaning house is to be prepared for unexpected or invited guests.

Ben wants Celeste to work for the added income, but he does not fully appreciate the fact that she is working two full-time jobs: teaching and homemaking. He will help her occasionally but feels this is definitely "her" work and is not ready to assume his share of the home responsibility. Celeste believes that child care, cooking, and cleaning should be equally divided chores.

Celeste wonders why Ben withholds attention, approval, and assistance. Though she receives little positive response from him, he expects her to be ready to make love whenever he wants it. "When I feel that we aren't on good terms," Celeste shared, "I can't enjoy that part of marriage. Ben expects me to turn my feelings off."

iNtuitives must be authentic and like to be credited for their ideas. Celeste, true to her type, prefers Ben to say something such as "I like your idea," "I appreciate how hard you work," and/or "I'm impressed with the insight and patience you have with the children."

Most INTJs like Ben struggle with saying thoughtful things or expressing appreciation or admiration for another's contributions because they don't expect to receive a lot of commendation for what they themselves do. However, they can learn to give strokes—if they have a patient teacher.

Celeste struggles just as hard with making logical decisions and handling mixed emotions. Ben can best help Celeste by not laughing condescendingly at her emotional decisions or saying they are ridiculous or juvenile.

As iNtuitives, both Ben and Celeste strive for a flawless marriage and perfect children—an unattainable goal. Ben wants the house to be immaculate at all times. Celeste is more concerned about people—especially their children—than maintaining a perfect house. Because Celeste dislikes disharmony, she will rarely mention her anxieties or defend herself.

Sharing the iNtuitive preference facilitated this couple's ability to understand their social differences and decision-making differences. Since both Ben and Celeste wanted perfection in themselves, parenting, and their relationship, their commitment led to achieving an adult-to-adult goal.

Encountering Social and Decision-making differences affects us on the job as well as in extended families on a daily basis, so it behooves us to expand our communication skills.

Extroversion, Sensing, and Feeling
ESFP (Daisy / Performer) and ESFJ (Zinnia / Host and Hostess)

Sharing the Sensing preference for gathering information through facts and figures seems to make for a good partnership, since spouses who think the same have fewer disagreements, especially if they have other temperamental traits in common—as Ben and Celeste do. However, this sameness may lead to competition to relieve the boredom, especially after the couple's initial goals have been reached or after their children are old enough not to need close parental supervision. Setting new goals each year offsets this trap.

Sensing people fall into routine ruts easily, which limits stimulation to communication. Some couples counteract indecision by writing on slips of paper various places to eat, things to do, and names of people to visit. They set aside one day or evening of the week to do something together; if neither has an idea for an activity, they just "draw from the hat" a slip of paper and do that. Most likely the ESFJ mate will want to know on Monday what will happen on Friday, whereas the ESFP mate will prefer to decide at the last minute.

Since ESFJs and ESFPs like to talk, they usually need practice in listening and editing their constant comments. Sensing people also function better with lots of information to stimulate communication. They prefer to solve problems as they bump into them—sometimes head-on, leaving them overwhelmed and powerless. In desperation, they may blame each other for being unaware of potential financial and family difficulties.

Since the majority of our population favor the Sensing preference, understanding the behavior of this temperament goes a long way in offering guidelines to the other 25 percent of temperaments in getting along with co-workers, neighbors, and extended family.

iNtuitive-Feeling and Sensing-Feeling
ENFJ (Poppy / Encourager) And ISFP (Rose / Sympathizer)

Like the majority of couples, an encourager and a sympathizer differ in at least two temperament preferences, so they have plenty to work on.

When an "idea" person and a "physical world" person put their heads together, the result is a clear picture. The iNtuitive will think of all the possibilities, and the Sensor will gather all the black-and-white facts. However, in an argument, they may get no place because they don't speak the same language. The same applies to work and family associations.

The iNtuitive will be wise to write down his or her ideas for the Sensing person to read and consider. Of course, the iNtuitive will likely forget some important facts, which the Sensing person cannot believe is possible. The iNtuitive will likely not enjoy taking care of financial records either, because working with figures is generally a boring chore to iNtuitives.

The Hands-on (Sensing) partner will be satisfied doing the same thing for years, while the iNtuitive may show a restlessness from time to time. When a goal is reached, an iNtuitive wants to try something new, although that is not always possible.

The ISFP wants to be appreciated for products and services. The ENFJ prefers recognition for ideas and contributions in helping people with emotional problems.

iNtuitives are likely to draw conclusions and make choices without a sufficient factual basis, especially when they feel pressured to make an immediate decision. They hate to admit that they do not know what they are expected to know. On the other hand, being a Feeling decision maker has both benefits and drawbacks.

Unique problems are created since the population in general accepts the view that it is somehow not masculine to be softhearted. A female is apt to feel insecure sharing decisions with a tenderhearted male who is easily hurt.

Learning to reach difficult decisions together so one person doesn't have the burden of making a final or unpleasant decision will move a couple to an adult-adult goal.

The Lifestyle difference (J and P) introduces some friction. The organized, Structured ENFJ will want to plan a schedule, get things done, and work all the time. The ISFP will want to put routine, mundane chores after recreation. Inevitable disagreements will disrupt the harmony they both crave.

A compatible relationship between any two people, despite their personality differences, results when understanding and appreciation are applied daily.

All Heart-Logic people need warmth, affection, approval, attention, and acceptance. These suggestions should help in work-related associations and in day-to-day exposure to softhearted people.

Complete Opposites

Complete opposites *can* make it! However, until each understands the other's strengths and appreciates the other's individual contributions, communication may be rough. The biggest adjustment will be in blending the sPontaneous-iNtuitive tendencies of one with the Structured-Sensing preferences of the other.

iNtuitive-sPontaneous and Sensing-Feeling-Structured
ENTP (Hibiscus / Powerful People Mover) and ISFJ (Tulip / Server)

The ISFJ will notice that the ENTP is constantly springing new ideas, making purchases, or investing in some "get rich quick" scheme, whereas the practical ISFJ prefers long-range, thorough planning based on factual information.

For example, the ENTP may want to take an extended trip but may rebel at the idea of making reservations along the way. Meeting deadlines does not appeal to ENTPs. ISFJs usually do not like surprises; they want to be ready for whatever happens. Since ENTPs enjoy excitement, planning things thoroughly destroys that inborn dimension.

Letting physical chores slide (for example, yard or car care, completing projects, etc.) will be a bone of contention for the ISFJ, who prefers to finish one project before beginning another and to take care of responsibilities before resting. No one can push or control an ENTP, so the best procedure is to offer simple non-offensive "I" statements of what he or she prefers to have done with a projected finish date, and let it stand at that.

ENTPs freely express their opinions—often controversial—to the dismay and embarrassment of ISFJs who prefer around-the-clock agreement and harmony. The flip side is that ENTPs are usually very demonstrative with their love and affection and exotic gifts. While ISFJs are a bit more private and practical in showing their love, they acknowledge good intentions and appreciate genuine private gestures of caring.

In my experience, ENTP teenagers present the most problems to parents who are Sensing and Structured. ENTPs want freedom—now! They trust themselves, but Sensing-Structured parents, teachers, and employers tend to resist granting freedom until teens prove they are responsible. This attitude creates a power struggle. The ENTP is comfortable with relationship risks and seems to be afraid of nothing or no one, which intensifies tensions. Even a four-year-old ENTP can rule the roost!

Introverted-sPontaneous-Thinking-iNtuitive
and Extroverted-Structured-Sensing-Feeler
INTP (Delphinium / Think-Tank Expert) and ESFJ (Zinnia / Host and Hostess)

Here is a beautiful case of total opposites who are attracted: An INTP is a private, profound Thinker who excels in the field of impersonal design and systems analysis. When paired with an ESFJ, a constant conversationalist who needs warmth, approval, and people all the time, concentrated attention is required to develop and maintain creative communication. This relationship parallels that of the ENTP-ISFJ in the previous example, and learning to blend the personalities will produce a solid, broad, and warm adult-to-adult relationship.

Often this combination occurs in a work relationship where the ESFJ is hired to take care of appointments, ordering supplies, and keeping records. Physicians, professors, engineers, CEOs, etc. look for this type of office assistant.

Obviously, an ESFJ's effervescence would get on an INTP's nerves as much as the INTP's solitary independence would come across as mysterious. As long as each considers the legitimate need for people with privacy needs, this difference can be positive. Transfer this to an ESFJ parent and an INTP teen. Pulling information from an INTP takes great patience and wisdom. It's best to use "I'm wondering" sentences.

iNtuitive possibilities paired with Sensing fact-finding couldn't be better. Acknowledging who has the best input for a specific decision is half the battle. An INTP is better at solving crisis problems, whereas an ESFJ shines when confronted with routine dilemmas in the immediate physical world. Such partners sometimes assume the other person is trying to be difficult, just to make waves, rather than being totally honest in airing their perspectives.

The ESFJ will likely have hurt feelings unless the INTP discovers how to modify generally critical opinions and assures the ESFJ that he or she is not the object under attack. On the other hand, the ESFJ is wise to run facts through the INTP's Thinking apparatus before making decisions. The INTP's protective Head-Logic decisions would keep the ESFJ from being walked on. By the same token, the ESFJ's practical real-world sensing powers would keep the iNtuitive's feet on the ground.

Any INTP needs to work at being warm, caring, and considerate, as well as trying to be a little more structured. This compromise is an adjustment to the ESFJ's desire for feedback to know beforehand when and where something will happen.

The ESFJ must learn to taper off conversation and build up a tolerance for criticism, working consciously toward releasing the INTP from an overload of people-business and family frivolity.

An INTP may be more competitive than an ESFJ appreciates. When an INTP remembers that an ESFJ has to have harmony and highly dislikes arguments, great strides will be made toward blending these two types.

Total opposites can possess the best of all worlds. When they succeed in achieving a good relationship through the art of creative compromise and skilled communication, they receive the highest honor: the Porcupine Award.

Thinking-Structured and Feeling-sPontaneous
ENTJ (Sunflower / Head Chief) and ENFP (Chrysanthemum / Catalyst)

Having two preferences in common eases tensions between partners, but their differences in decision-making methods and lifestyle offer plenty of challenge, which these types like and need.

Sharing Extroversion aids communication, and their mutual preference for iNtuitive information gathering provides enjoyment and understanding. Both partners need several goals and prefer a complex life, but friction will likely occur over decision making.

ENFPs want approval and people-input before making decisions, while ENTJs make their decisions fully expecting approval afterwards. ENTJs trust their own decisions the most, whereas ENFPs will likely feel steamrolled unless they courageously insist on contributing to final decisions.

Although ENFPs come across as very confident, with feelings of steel, the opposite is true. They are quite sensitive, especially when their ideas or emotions are being ignored or rejected. An ENTJ is wise to slow the process somewhat in order to be gentle and considerate and to verbalize approval and acceptance regularly.

In parenting, an ENTJ assumes he/she is in charge and will expect children to obey quickly and remember rules. An ENFP will be less strict or even inconsistent, because this type dislikes rules and schedules for anyone. ENFPs usually do not like humdrum duties or meeting arbitrary deadlines, a tendency that may grate against an ENTJ mate's desire for order. Yet, ENTJs are not usually crazy about taking care of menial, sensory-oriented tasks either.

Although ENTJs prefer to delegate assignments, offering physical assistance greatly encourages ENFPs and can make mundane duties tolerable and more fun. ENTJs want to be appreciated for wise, strategic, and practical decisions, in contrast to ENFPs, who want to assist those who struggle with emotional emergencies, giving generously of time, money, and effort (which ENTJs will deem impractical at times).

ENFPs like to play and have dozens of ideas for activities, especially outdoors. They prefer to gather information at the last minute, when there is no time left to change it, then make a decision.

ENTJs also like to play, but preferably after work is done. They detest indecision, wanting plans to be firmed up ahead of time so that no time or energy is lost.

ENFPs and ENTJs, numbering a mere five percent of the general population, wield much influence as they head up and serve on committees. With great charisma and optimistic leadership, they use their natural expertise in openly communicating new ideas with confidence. They're cooperative and fun to observe as they move easily from Plan A to Plan B to put their schemes for improvement into practical use.

Structured-Sensing-Feeling and iNtuitive-sPontaneous-Feeling
ISFJ (Tulip / Server) and INFP (Portulaca / Idealist)

ISFJ Roy and INFP Wilma share Introversion and Heart-Logic. Combining tender-hearted introverts is challenging since conversation is not easy and each is very sensitive to disagreements. But without assistance in how to value each other, they'll struggle privately and both will be confused regarding their relationship. They will have to intentionally resist the tendency of a child-child relationship rather than an adult-adult one.

"For a long time, I really believed that I didn't love Roy and didn't want to live with him anymore," Wilma explained. "Now, I know that's not true. I really do love him very much, and I want to share the rest of my life with him."

Wilma and Roy had been together more than 20 years and had several adult children. After being cooped up for so long, the idealist Wilma craved space. Roy, being a hands-on and structured person, liked physical routine and disliked change. He wanted them to do everything together as a couple.

"When I'd escape to the basement to fold clothes, there he'd be by my side," Wilma complained. "If I was washing dishes, he'd come up from behind and kiss my neck and touch me. This gave me the creeps. He always wanted to go shopping with me and loved to help choose my clothes. I just felt crowded and wanted to be alone.

"He took my need for space personally and tried to put guilt trips on me when I wouldn't respond to his verbal affection. It got so that my favorite time of day was when he would leave for work, and my worst moment was when he returned. Yet, Roy's a very fine person. I admire him in many ways. I just needed space and spontaneity in my life.

"I was so bored with my routine and who I had become that I didn't like him either. It seemed like I could do nothing well. I longed to be somebody. He would assure me that I was somebody—his life partner—but that only angered me. I wanted to be special to more than just him. With professional help, Roy learned to back off and not demand my total attention or affection. He even learned to graciously withhold what he really wanted to give.

"A lot of Roy's behavior was a reaction to my needing to become 'Wilma,' not just Roy's wife and the kids' mom. I still get really scared when I realize that Roy needs me to be his wife, just as much as I need to be more than that. I don't know how to work that out. I need to be my own person, free to have needs, feelings, opinions, interest, likes, and dislikes. What if my needs infringe on his—and his on mine?

"I'm going to be me, and maybe Roy won't like that person. He said last night, 'If I don't like the new you, I'll pack up and be out like a shot, because I know there's happiness out there for me.'

"Right now, I love Roy more than I have ever loved him—but in a whole new way. I'm just beginning to realize how important he is to me, and I want to spend the rest of my life in the world we've built together. But I won't be happy in that world if it's not okay to be me."

Separating would have been difficult for both of these introverted softhearted people. Clashing over routine versus spontaneity became apparent after all the forced structure of raising children and having to meet deadlines subsided. Wilma didn't find out who she was until after all their children were out of the nest. The simple understanding of their different lifestyle needs is all they needed to solve their problem.

sPontaneous-iNtuitive and Structured-Sensing
ENFP (Chrysanthemum / Catalyst) Mother and ISFJ (Tulip / Server) Daughter

This mother-teenaged daughter situation illustrates a successful resolution of conflict through understanding their inborn differences:

"I've been aware that Cindy and I are vastly different since she was a little tyke. She behaved differently than her dad and I attempted to teach her. She was not very friendly and cried a lot about insignificant things. We wondered if she might have a problem understanding directions and expressing herself. We had no clue that our differing personalities created the conflict in our home.

"Now I can appreciate the fact that Cindy prefers to receive instructions in steps rather than hearing about the overall outcome that I expect. I also understand why she is overwhelmed with the conversation at our house—her dad and brother are also Extroverted, iNtuitive, and sPontaneous as I am. Cindy is indeed outnumbered!

"Cindy is inclined to keep things neat and wants to know exactly when we are going to leave and return, rather than just jumping up and going, as we all prefer.

"We are now able to enjoy each other's uniqueness instead of having it be a source of constant irritation. Since a lot of the friction is gone, we find that we can often laugh over those very differences that used to erupt into arguments. Cindy's self-esteem has improved since all of us by action and word give her deliberate approval and respect for her family contributions. We value how she's been designed. She adds a gracious dimension to our family."

Riding Out the Storm

How very important it is to know how to adjust to outside influences. Every person we meet leaves a mark and requires some compromise as we interact. In a flower garden we know that fierce winds and inclement weather force many plants to become stronger and develop a better root system. The elements of nature also clean away ugly debris. So too, climate changes can benefit and improve our garden of human relationships involving partners, children, extended family, work, club associations, and neighbors.

Good luck to you, reader, as you utilize this communication skill that can release fresh seed-ideas to unlock understanding and appreciation for blending personalities and getting along with everyone. (Learn more at ruthmcrobertsward.com.)

This amateur ENFJ gardener, who is also a veteran believer, trusts that the next and final chapter will graft temperament, type, and personality into a personal relationship with the Master Gardener who values and equips his children—the Servers, Hostesses, Organizers, Encouragers, Emphasizers, Think-Tank Experts, People Movers, Head Chiefs, Sympathizers, Conscientious Workers, Performers, Unstoppables, Rescuers, Idealists, Catalysts, and Sympathizers—to serve, influence, and improve all communities.

Hopefully, based on all we've discussed, these final thoughts will serve as an open window to a deeper understanding of God's love and his enabling and purpose for every personality as we "bloom where we're planted" in God's unique and lovely garden.

Relying on God to inspire us and give us patience with others and ourselves resembles the fresh, warm breeze after a storm. I've attempted to be carefully open-minded and not dogmatic, aware that everyone's level of spiritual understanding differs based on church and family background, schooling, and personal experiences.

CHAPTER 10

Meeting God's Expectations: Enjoying the Garden

He has showed you, O man, what is good.
And what does the LORD require of you?
To act justly and to love mercy and to walk humbly with your God.
Micah 6:8

Once people discover how wonderfully and intricately they are designed, many naturally want to get better acquainted with the Designer and thank him.

After learning how uniquely she and others had been designed, Eloise became interested for the first time in her 29 years in the magnitude of God's love in sending Jesus to provide the path to God. She expressed it succinctly: "If God did all this for me and loved me when I was so unlovable and not the least interested in him or spiritual things, he must have a will for me. How do I discover it?"

Understanding God's Will

"What does God want me to do?" Just as parents yearn to hear that question from their child, so God delights to hear it from his children. When we know who we are and whose we are, discovering God's will is not such a mystery. Important truths and guidelines about how God works and what he desires for humankind are revealed in scripture. Overall, God wants to give us hope, peace, love, joy, and purpose.

God's Love Is Unconditional and Unearned

The Scriptures state clearly that every person is a "somebody" who has been redeemed because of the Creator's love. My personal trek toward healthy self-esteem is directly related to discovering how unconditionally God loves me. If God created me and considers me his treasure, friend, co-worker, and ambassador, how could I ever look down on myself and consider myself a bothersome mistake?

We can never earn God's love no matter how hard we try. The way to please God is by accepting his gift of unconditional love. Though earthly parents may put their children in bondage by setting performance standards, God does not deal with us from such a conditional love base.

God supremely loves everyone—believer and nonbeliever alike. This is difficult for finite beings to comprehend. It's sobering, but also releasing, to understand that God will love us no more after 10 years of adult service than he does when we are spiritual infants. There is no way to make points with God or to get him to love us less.

God's Plan Is All-Wise and Caring

Some people resent and stay angry with God for years or reject God entirely because they blame him when life presents hurdles. We have no reason to get mad at God because his children misbehave. That's like saying, "Mom, I'm mad at you because my brother hit me."

Rodney was upset with God for not answering his prayers. "For the last two years I've not enjoyed my work. I've had stomach pains and headaches. I've asked God to show me what's wrong with me and make me like my job, but he hasn't answered my prayers."

When we are tuned in for one answer only, we tie God's hands. I suggested to Rodney: "You've told God what to do—make you like your job. Perhaps he has another assignment for you that would suit you better."

This INTJ had exhausted the challenge of his hands-on job but blamed his unhappiness on God. Dealing with ill-fitted or worn-out careers or jobs is a common experience, especially for mid-life iNtuitives. The problem is often our own making, and certainly nothing to blame on God. In fact, our dissatisfaction—restlessness—may be God's way of telling us to get on with what he intended. This gentleman quit his mostly Sensing noisy job and became a director for a non-profit organization that suited his Introverted, iNtuitive design perfectly.

God's Way Is All-Powerful but Unfathomable

Questioning God is a popular pastime: "Why doesn't God stop terrorism and war?" "Why does God allow innocent people to suffer?" "Why did God let my little girl die?" "Why doesn't God stop drunk drivers?"

"What do you expect God to do?" I might ask the last questioner. "Keep people from taking a drink or restrain them from getting behind the wheel of an automobile?"

"Yes," most would agree. "If God is as powerful as the Bible claims, he could stop unnecessary pain and suffering."

If that's how we expect God to act, we would also have to be willing to find ourselves pushed out of bed on a cold, rainy day after a too-late night, being forced against our will to attend church. Few of us would vote for that! There are restrictions many people request for others but do not want for themselves.

Some teachers claim that God is helpless and cannot control events. But my pastor-husband says, "God has as much power now as he had when he created this world or designed humans. It's not that he can't manipulate; but God chooses instead not to use the power he has. God won't violate our free will, even when we do terrible things. This ensures that our love toward him is voluntary."

God does not send death, destruction, and sorrow, but may use humanly uncontrollable elements—floods, tornadoes, draughts, fire—to gain our attention, purify, and strengthen. God has promised to help us endure unpleasant and painful experiences.

We may not live long enough to witness the long-range benefit of our personal trials, but in faith we can trust God to use our personalities, influence, and service

God's Threefold Expectation

Faithfulness

God first calls us to be faithful—not perfect nor even prestigious and successful. Since he designed us, the Creator certainly knows best how to empower and direct our lives. But God will not force his will on anyone.

Because God is totally faithful to his people, he expects our faithfulness in return. The Lord expects that our right relationship with him will produce a like relationship with our fellowman. Meaningful worship of God and ethical conduct toward other people go together.

Sincerity

God also expects sincerity of spirit, not commercialized religion or a mechanical form of worship. We need to beware of the temptation to manipulate God rather than worship him. It is a faulty assumption to consider that what we do in church or community places God in our debt, so that when we ask him for something he is duty-bound to grant it. No one can bargain with God.

Prayerful Obedience

God's third basic requirement has two parts: prayer and obedience. Even as we do God's will, God expects us to lay requests before him and allow him to work in our hearts and the hearts of those with whom we have contact.

Since prayer is the most natural product of real love for God, the desire to pray is evidence that Jesus' commandment to love God has taken root and is growing within us. If we do not want to talk with God, can the idea that we love him have any basis in reality?

"In the morning, O Lord, you hear my voice; in the morning I lay my requests before you and wait in expectation" (Ps. 5:3). Until we lay our requests before God regularly, we will not discover the loving companionship he has in mind for us.

Ascertaining God's Will Through Our Strengths

Some very conscientious people assume that God's ideal is to force them to do what is unpleasant or hard. Speaking to or serving others regarding the spiritual life requires wisdom and courage for all personalities. God understands who we are and what we can do to honor him.

Yvonne shared: "I was always a disappointment to my dad because I was, and still am, a timid person and find it difficult to talk to or help anyone I don't know. Therefore, I've always felt that I have short-changed God as well."

I have no doubt that Jesus would reply to Yvonne, "I only ask that you come to me. I will give you courage to share your influence in your own special way through words or service."

In addition to their physical beauty, flowers make distinctive contributions. Some exude an unusual fragrance that aids pollination by luring honeybees to their nectar. Others produce edible leaves or seeds, useful oils, or herbs for cooking. Still others possess medicinal qualities in their roots or stems. So, too, does each person have a particular contribution to make in building God's kingdom. Although the terms talents, fruit of the Spirit, and spiritual gifts may be confusing, each has its distinctive function.

God is not unreasonable. He knows our physical, spiritual, and mental limitations and provides opportunities that coincide with our inborn and achieved abilities. Many people are surprised to discover the magnitude of their unique gifts to the world.

An aptitude or skill that one is born with or acquires through training and practice—such as musical ability, writing, mechanical abilities, sports, finances, counseling, speaking, dancing, art, crafts, gardening, woodworking, etc.—is considered a natural or developed talent.

In his wisdom and mercy, God has endowed certain people with the raw material to excel and become masters in their fields. Consider Handel, Beethoven, and Bach, whose musical works have contributed significantly to both listening pleasure and meaningful worship.

In the latter realm, we are equally indebted to disciplined theological scholars who possess the intelligence, insight, and ability to study the Scriptures in their original languages and cultural setting and then provide modern translations for the various world cultures.

Quick analysis of other learned or natural talents would divulge many proofs of God's special enabling and "talenting." However, many people are so aware of their frailties, failures, and inadequacies that they overlook their subtle yet significant potential for contributions.

Behind-the-scenes workers who consider themselves ordinary are seldom acknowledged publicly for their service or ideas, but their contributions are as marvelous as any well-known person. C.S. Lewis, a popular writer, declared that no one is ordinary. In God's sight, everyone is as valuable as the next one. Faithfully doing what we do best and maintaining a kind and helpful attitude is extraordinary.

Fruit of the Spirit

Through the Holy Spirit, as Galatians 5:22-23 records, God equips believers with love, joy, peace, patience, kindness, goodness, faithfulness, gentleness, and self-control.

These attitudes develop from our personal relationship with and dependence upon God. As believers, then, we have access to all these qualities at any time through prayer. When these characteristics accompany or back up our words, attitudes, and actions, nonbelievers take notice, are impressed with our demeanor, and are often thereby attracted to our Master.

First Corinthians 13:1-3 clearly outlines the importance of servers' attitude of love: "If I speak in the tongues of men and of angels, but have not love, I am only a resounding gong or a clanging cymbal. If I have the gift of prophecy and can fathom all mysteries and all knowledge, and if I have a faith that can move mountains, but have not love, I am nothing. If I give all I possess to the poor and surrender my body to the flames, but have not love, I gain nothing."

The Holy Spirit reveals opportunities for sharing our personal friendship with God. He teaches us the priority of people and encourages us as we relate to others in love. Depending on spiritual gifts enables us to reach out wisely to those who need physical and spiritual assistance. All through the Bible, without respect to temperament or special gifting from the Holy Spirit, we are urged to share our personal experiences of depending on the Lord.

Enjoying God's Garden

A healthy, beautiful array of blooms—minus weeds—pleases any gardener. In human terms, God is the gardener and we are the flowers. Each of us is unique as we reflect upon and influence our neighbor-plants and mutually experience changes in the weather, sunless days, and all the enemies a garden endures.

We all have potential contributions to make to our immediate neighbors and the rest of the world as we share a common goal: to make the world a better place. Understanding temperaments—ours and others—raises personal self-esteem and improves our appreciation for everyone. The resulting harmony among the flowers in our human garden gives God great pleasure.

Ephesians 3:16-19 is a wonderful passage to conclude *How to Get Along with Everyone by Blending Personalities.* "I pray that out of his glorious riches he may strengthen you with power through his Spirit in your inner being, so that Christ may dwell in your hearts through faith. And I pray that you, being rooted and established in love, may have power, together with all the saints, to grasp how wide and long and high and deep is the love of Christ, and to know this love that surpasses knowledge—that you may be filled to the measure of all the fullness of God."

CPSIA information can be obtained
at www.ICGtesting.com
Printed in the USA
BVHW040018120819
555624BV00028B/5330/P

9 781635 280838